BRIGHT NOTES

THE BEGGAR'S OPERA
BY
JOHN GAY

Intelligent Education

INFLUENCE PUBLISHERS

Nashville, Tennessee

BRIGHT NOTES: The Beggar's Opera
www.BrightNotes.com

ISBN: 978-1-645422-70-9 (Paperback)
ISBN: 978-1-645422-71-6 (eBook)

Published in accordance with the U.S. Copyright Office Orphan Works and Mass Digitization report of the register of copyrights, June 2015.

Originally published by Monarch Press.
Steven H. Gale, 1974
2019 Edition published by Influence Publishers.

Interior design by Lapiz Digital Services. Cover Design by Thinkpen Designs.

Printed in the United States of America.

Library of Congress Cataloging-in-Publication Data forthcoming.
Names: Intelligent Education
Title: BRIGHT NOTES: The Beggar's Opera
Subject: STU004000 STUDY AIDS / Book Notes

CONTENTS

INTRODUCTION TO JOHN GAY

Of the three major periods in British drama (Elizabethan, Restoration and eighteenth century, and contemporary), the Restoration/eighteenth century era is usually considered the age of comedy. In addition it is characterized as a time of innovation and variety. John Gay's eighteenth-century comedy masterpiece, *The Beggar's Opera* (1728), is especially representative of its period because of its humor. Without a doubt the most popular drama written during the hundred years between 1700 and 1800, *The Beggar's Opera* is, moreover, with William Congreve's *The Way of the World* (1700), one of the only two plays of any real artistic worth to be composed in England from 1700 to 1773. Gay's work has since become a literary "classic" throughout the world, while still retaining its popularity with the general public, theatre-goers and readers alike.

The basis of the play's success rests on three factors: its artistic merit; its originality (this is in part measured by the number of later dramas which clearly display the influence of its innovations); and its pervasive humor. This last element is the most important single aspect of the play, yet, like any piece of lasting value, *The Beggar's Opera* does not exist solely because it entertains people; the humor also serves as a medium for carrying the author's meaning - social **satire** which is applicable in all countries at all times.

CHRONOLOGY OF IMPORTANT DATES

1685-John Gay born

1708-First publication, *Wine.* Meets Pope

1712-First play, *The Mohocks*

1713-Becomes secretary of the Scriblerus Club

1714-*The Shepherd's Week*

1716-*Trivia*

1720-Financial difficulties

1723-Appointed Commissioner of State Lottery

1727-*Fables*

1728-*The Beggar's Opera*

1732-Gay dies

BACKGROUND: EIGHTEENTH-CENTURY BRITISH DRAMA

Overview

The year 1700 has been considered the end of major dramatic endeavor in England, previous to a resurgence of the theatre in the modern era, because the Reverend Jeremy Collier's scathing attack, *A Short View of the Immorality and Profaneness of the English Stage*, was published just two years previously and 1700 marked both the death of John Dryden and the retirement of William Congreve. Reasons given for the general decline in the English theatre after 1700 have included: the unfavorable physical conditions of the playhouses; the expansion of the middle-class element in the audience which refused to tolerate the "immorality" of the Restoration while imposing its own dull lack of taste on the stage; and the Licensing Act of 1737 which virtually stifled dramatic originality (ironically, though, leading to a Shakespearean revival and refinement in acting techniques). In fact, Sir Ifor Evans sums up this attitude toward the eighteenth century by saying, in *A Short History of English Drama* (Boston, 1965), "It cannot be denied that the eighteenth century and the first fifty years of the nineteenth were, with the exception of only some half-a-dozen names, a dreary period as far as dramatic authorship is concerned."[1] At best this statement is an oversimplification.

At the beginning of the century, Congreve's *The Way of the World* (1700) brought down the curtain on the Restoration as the greatest of Restoration comedies of manners and wit. The turn toward "sentimental comedy" was signaled seven years later when George Farquhar moved the setting of *The Beaux' Stratagem* out of the city of London and into the country, focusing his attention on the moral orientation of his characters in their new surroundings - Richard Steele's 1723 drama, *The Conscious*

Lovers, is the epitome of the **genre** in full bloom. From the mid-seventies Oliver Goldsmith's *She Stoops to Conquer* and Richard Brinsley Sheridan's *The Rivals and The School for Scandal* stand as paragons of the best "laughing" comedies ever written for the British stage.

While the playwriting did decline as the century advanced, especially after 1737, there were numerous other important events which took place between 1700 and 1777, including John Gay's inventive *The Beggar's Opera* (1728), Joseph Addison's classically constructed tragedy *Cato* (1713), and the counterpart of the sentimental movement in comedy, sentimental tragedy, represented by George Lillo's *The London Merchant* (1731). Generally speaking, as the century advanced the plays tended to be of a more **didactic** nature and originality in the theatre was concentrated on technical aspects of staging rather than in "creative" playwriting. Thus, in spite of the dampening effect of the Licensing Act, Charles Macklin and David Garrick brought a new style of acting to the English theatre and Garrick, Ferdinand Bibiena, and Philippe de Loutherbourg contributed technical advances in staging.

Theatres

The most important of the twenty playhouses which functioned in London in the eighteenth century were the Queen's Haymarket, built by John Vanbrugh in 1705 and renamed King's after George I's ascension to the throne (it could seat about 1,300 by 1735); the Theatre Royal in Lincoln's Inn Fields; and the Theatre Royal or Drury Lane Theatre in Bridges Street. The two Theatres Royal, originally authorized by Charles II in 1660 when the monarchy was restored, underwent some changes over the years, with the Lincoln's Inn Fields Theatre

Royal being torn down and replaced by the 1,400-seat Covent Garden in 1732 and Drury Lane being expanded from a capacity of about 1,200 to facilities for seating nearly 1,800 spectators. Dorset Garden, another important Restoration playhouse, was demolished in 1709.

Technical developments included Garrick's introduction of a new French lighting system in 1765 which provided for color effects, the Italian Bibiena's scena per angolo which allowed more realistic dimensional presentation by discarding the concept of a central axis in dressing the stage, and the Swiss de Loutherbourg's painted gauze "transparencies" which permitted a single backdrop to be used for two different scenic effects, depending on the positioning of the light source.

Audience And Sentimental Comedy

Notwithstanding the technical and physical improvements and the enlarged middle-class audiences of lesser royalty, doctors, clergy, and merchants, the rowdy actions of Restoration spectators were still in force and the interiors of the theatres were periodically destroyed (on the average of every five years), as a result of displeasure with actors or plays, as the patrons vented their feelings on the furnishings. The most important effect of the audience, though, was the type of drama it was willing to support, and the type of drama that it was most willing to support, starting with Colley Cibber's *Love's Last Shift* in 1696, was that which obviously appealed to the audience's emotions - sentimental comedy.

The characteristics of sentimental comedy are moralizing, emotional release, and the presentation of exemplary characters. According to F. T. Wood's definition of sentimental comedy,[2]

5

a sympathetic audience is essential for the acceptance of drama which moves from the ridicule of type characters in the previous century to the near tragic in depicting the lives of eighteenth-century characters - with the consequence of concentrating on individualized problems that tend to involve human nature as opposed to social mannerisms, thereby approaching the definition of tragedy. The result is a morally **didactic** theatre which emphasizes the innate goodness of man (a positive point of view implying man's perfectibility). Arthur Sherbo claims in *English Sentimental Drama* (East Lansing, 1959) that "debased," "artificial" drama of a sentimental nature is incapable of producing anything of literary value, for it is limited by its attempt to appeal to the audience's emotions through an improbable plot weakened by overstressing the moral element which always rests on a belief in man's essential goodness. John Loftis' study, *Comedy and Society from Congreve to Fielding* (Stanford, 1959), finds the term "sentimental comedy" inaccurate and stresses the increasing economic rivalry between the aristocracy and the emerging merchant class after the end of the war with France in 1710 as the foundation for the genre's popularity.

Tragedy

The character of tragedy underwent changes during the eighteenth century, too. Addison's *Cato*, emphasizing the formal standards devised by Aristotle and Horace, is the best piece to come out of the period, while Nicholas Rowe produced inferior work after the same models. Lillo's forerunner of domestic tragedy, *The London Merchant* (1731), and John Home's later dramas, however, reflected the same shift in popular taste which was determining the direction in which comedy was evolving, for Lillo's psychologically oriented piece involved an interest in the individual and an effort to teach moral lessons to his audience by appealing to their sentiments.

Licensing Act Of 1737

The single element which most profoundly affected eighteenth-century English drama was the Licensing Act of 1737. Early in the period there had been a short flurry of dramatic experimentation, but this was effectively curtailed when the number of legitimate playhouses in London was reduced to two (Drury Lane and Covent Garden - when there had been as many as five theatres in simultaneous operation), and all public entertainment was brought under the control of the Lord Chamberlain.

Since everything to be performed first had to be approved by the Lord Chamberlain, the type of drama to be acted was in effect predetermined. Although there were productions put on under false pretenses, such as supposed art exhibits or concerts, the majority of plays were "safe" in that they conformed to the Lord Chamberlain's dictates (which were prescribed by Prime Minister Robert Walpole). Interestingly, this also led to a Shakespearean revival since Shakespeare was considered "safe." In the forty years between 1660 and 1700 eighteen of Shakespeare's plays had been acted - in the next forty years, from 1700 to 1741, thirty Shakespearean dramas were produced, including the twenty-seven under Garrick's aegis as manager of Drury Lane (1747–1776) which accounted for a combined total of over 1,000 performances. In fact, at both Drury Lane and Covent Garden fifteen percent of the comedies and thirty percent of the tragedies seen during Garrick's tenure were Shakespeare's.

An additional and perhaps unlooked for result of the Licensing Act was an improvement in acting techniques. Because artistic originality was prohibited from expressing itself in playwriting, other aspects of the theatre became proportionately more important and together with better staging conditions and Shakespearean roles to play, this brought about a break with the more declamatory acting style which was currently popular. First Charles Macklin (initially in the role of Shylock in a 1741 production of *The Merchant of Venice*) and then Garrick led the movement for naturalism in acting. Indeed, Garrick, usually declared the greatest of all English actors and said to have been able to perform ninety parts at a moment's notice, was well-known for his subtle portrayal of Shakespearean characters. Garrick also was responsible for a reform banning spectators from sitting on the stage - almost an act of self-protection, since it was not uncommon for members of the audience to disrupt a play by insulting or actually assaulting the cast.

Laughing Comedy

The most productive part of the eighteenth century in terms of quality were those years between 1773 and 1777. Hugh Kelly's *False Delicacy* (1768) and Richard Cumberland's *The West Indian* (1771) demonstrated that sentimental comedy was still an imposing factor on the English stage, but the new "laughing" comedy of Goldsmith and Sheridan was strong opposition. Goldsmith's *The Good-Natured Man* (1768) and *She Stoops to Conquer* (1773) are related to the comedy of the earlier years of the century in their retention of the sentimental assumption of man's basic goodness, yet the dramatist's mode of expression is much more closely allied to the witty ridicule of the funnier comedies of manners. *The Rivals* (1775) and *The School for Scandal* (1777) by Sheridan carried on Goldsmith's challenge of what Sheridan derided as "the goddess of the woeful countenance - the Sentimental Muse." Lydia, clearly a typical sentimental heroine, is held up to ridicule in the first play, and Joseph Surface, the "man of sentiment" who is revealed as a most flagrant villain, is the subject of attack in the second.

With Goldsmith's death and Sheridan's withdrawal from playwriting in favor of his position as manager of Drury Lane, British drama had exhausted its genius. Not for another hundred years would there be anything important written for the English stage.

LIFE AND WORKS OF JOHN GAY

John Gay was born on Joy Street in Barnstaple, Devonshire on June 30, 1685, the youngest son of a youngest son. It was here in this middle-class atmosphere that the future dramatist first heard of Newgate Prison - through the tales of his Aunt Martha, who had been bankrupt in a New World business endeavor and consequently spent several years in Newgate.

The young Gay became interested in poetry through the efforts of the Reverend Robert Luck, his Barnstaple Grammar Schoolmaster, who wrote poetry and directed the yearly Barnstaple Grammar School play, but his interest was not allowed to develop for a number of years due to the death of both of his parents in 1694. He was sent first to live with his Uncle Thomas Gay and then upon his uncle's death seven years later he was apprenticed to William Ayre, a silk mercer in London. Fortunately, Gay's fondness for reading interfered with his learning the silk trade properly, and after completing only half of his apprenticeship he was released by his master in 1706.

Gay returned to Barnstaple for a short time, then moved back to London in 1707 where he became secretary to Aaron Hill (who was later to become a manager of the Drury Lane Theatre). With Hill's help, Gay published his first poem, "Wine," in 1708, a mediocre imitation of Milton, though of sufficient quality to be pirated. Hill also introduced the young poet to the society world of London coffee-house wits and authors, among whom was Alexander Pope, who encouraged him to take up playwriting. Gay's maiden effort was a farce called *The Mohocks* which was never acted, though its publication in 1712 helped establish the dramatist's reputation with Pope's circle and led the following year to his becoming secretary of the Scriblerus Club (whose membership included Pope, Jonathan Swift, Dr. John Arbuthnot, Thomas Parnell and Joseph Spence). In addition Gay published three minor works during 1713, two poems, "Rural Sports" (January 13) and "The Fan" (December 8), and another drama, *The Wife of Bath*, which ran for three nights.

The author's initial popular success, though, came with the publication of "The Shepherd's Week" on April 15, 1714 which so pleased Oliver Goldsmith that he wrote that Gay "has hit the true spirit of pastoral poetry. In fact, he more resembles Theocritus than any other English pastoral writer whatsoever." The dramatist's first theatrical success, *The What d'ye Call It*, was performed a year later. The **ballad** "T'was when the seas were roaring," music supposedly by Handel, was one of the highlights of the drama - a tune which appears again as "Air XXVIII" in *The Beggar's Opera*.

"Trivia," a vivid description of "The Art of Walking the Streets of London," appeared in 1716, but Gay suffered both financial and literary reversals for a number of years thereafter. He wrote *Three Hours after Marriage*, a comedy satirizing the works of Josiah Woodward, John Dennis, and Colley Cibber, in collaboration with Pope and Arbuthnot, only to be embarrassed by a riot at the theatre on the opening night and Joseph Addison's charge that the play was obscene; in an attempt to earn some badly needed money he published the unproduced pastoral tragedy *Dione* in 1720; and he even resorted to a bit of hack-writing with other lesser poets composing lyrics for Queen Esther, Handel's first English oratorio. Finally, in 1723, Gay achieved a degree of financial security when he was given a post as commissioner of state lotteries at 150 pounds a year and simultaneously obtained lodgings at Whitehall through the efforts of the Earl of Lincoln

Freed from the necessity of earnings a living by his writing, Gay now could work on his creations more leisurely and under less pressure. *The Captives*, which opened at the Drury Lane early in 1724, was a conventional tragedy of the type that he had previously ridiculed in *The What d'ye Call It*, but the piece appealed to Queen Caroline. Gay's next truly popular success did not come until March, 1727, though, when his *The Fables* were published. *The Fables*, ostensibly written for Queen Caroline's four-year-old son, Prince William Augustus, brought their author both fame and riches, yet they did not bring what he most sought - Court favor - for when the list of preferments appeared in October, 1727, Gay was awarded the minor post of Gentleman-Usher to two-year-old Princess Louisa at 150 pounds a year. Incensed by this slight (see his poem "The Hare and Many Friends" for his view of his relations with the Court), Gay declined the appointment, disassociating himself with the Court and thereby allowing him to turn his attentions to the politically scathing **satire**, *The Beggar's Opera* (written at Pope's estate in Twickenham), which opened three months later on January 29, 1728.

The Beggar's Opera was the high point of Gay's career. The inferior sequel, *Polly*, was suppressed on Prime Minister Walpole's insistence by the Lord Chamberlain in December, 1728, although it is less politically damning than its original. *Acis and Galatea*, an operetta based on Handel's score and written ten years earlier, was performed in 1731 and the second series of *The Fables and Achilles*, another opera, were written in 1732. Two plays written during the final years of his life, *The Distress'd Wife* and *The Rehearsal at Goatham*, were published posthumously.

While in London making arrangements for the production of *Achilles* at the Covent Garden, Gay died on December 4, 1732 after a three-day illness diagnosed as inflammation of the bowels. After lying in state for nineteen days, his body was buried under a bust by Rysbrock in Westminster Abbey next to the tomb of Chaucer on December 23. On his monument were inscribed two epitaphs, one by Pope:

Of manners gentle, of affections mild; In with, a man; simplicity, a child: With native humor temp'ring virtuous rage, Form'd to delight at once and lash the age: Above temptation, in a low estate, And uncorrupted, ev'n among the great: A safe companion, and an easy friend, Unblamed through life, lamented in thy end. These are they honours! not that here thy bust Is mix'd with heroes, or with kings thy dust; But that the worthy and the good shall say, Striking their pensive bosoms - Here lies Gay.

Gay's own **epitaph**, written when he was seriously ill three years earlier, was also inscribed on the monument:

Life is a jest; and all things show it. I thought so once; but now I know it.

THE BEGGAR'S OPERA

INTRODUCTION

. . . .

BACKGROUND

The Beggar's Opera, a three-act "**ballad** opera" divided into forty-five scenes and an introduction and containing a total of 69 airs, was the first of its **genre** to be performed, but it drew on several traditions. Obviously it is a political and social **satire**, comparing the Court to the criminal underworld. In addition it is a "Newgate pastoral," a combination of pastoral conventions placed in a Newgate setting and meant to **burlesque** the form of Italian opera.

A pastoral was originally a poem treating the rustic life of shepherds. From this **convention** Gay borrowed the subject of the lower classes for the purpose of creating what William Empson (see Some Versions of the Pastoral) terms literary inversion, a device used in "putting the complex into the simple." Gay also took advantage of the use of songs in the pastoral tradition to cash in on the great popularity of Scottish and English **ballads** in the eighteenth century.

Furthermore, the Newgate setting allowed the dramatist to utilize underworld characters of the type currently drawing so much interest. Among those individuals his contemporaries talked about daily were Jonathan Blake (whose trial at the Old Baily in 1725 Gay celebrated in the poem "Newgate's Garland"),[3] Jonathan Wild, and Jack Sheppard. Wild, the prototype for Peachum, actually gathered together a huge gang of thieves, pickpockets, highwaymen, and so forth, to supply him with stolen goods which he either "fenced" or returned to the rightful owner for a large reward. Like Peachum, he readily gave information against members of his own organization if he felt they represented a threat because they knew too much, or because they demanded a larger share of the profits, or because they tried to assemble a rival group of criminals, and all told was responsible for the hanging of approximately 100 people, thus gaining recognition as the "Thief-taker General of Great Britain and Ireland." Blake was one of his victims, and Wild also informed on Sheppard before he himself was hanged at Tyburn on May 24, 1725, on a charge of returning stolen property to its owner without notifying the police (ironically, the loot came from a theft for which he had been legally acquitted).

Jack Sheppard's sensational exploits fired the public's imagination. His daring escapes from prison and his defiance of the criminal laws so appealed to people upset with the brutal punishments meted out to criminals (hanging, beheadings, disembowelings, whippings, and imprisonment in the hulks) and the activities of Wild's gang of cutthroats, that the crowds kidnapped his body and took it to an ale house in Long Acre after he was hanged in November, 1725. On November 17, 1725 *The Daily Journal* reported that the arrival of a bailiff to procure the body for burial "occasioned a great Riot" and a company of Guards, bayonets fixed, had to be called out to escort the casket to its St. Martin's Fields resting place. The following year saw the printing of numerous versions of the "Life and Adventures" of Wild and of Sheppard, including an account by Daniel Defoe (which Fielding later followed in writing his 1743 book on Wild).

In his **burlesque** of Italian opera, a form which remained extremely popular in spite of continued denouncements by the better critics, Gay wove all of these threads together. There was a long history of opera on the English stage, going back to the masques of Jonson and Milton prior to the Interregnum. These were succeeded by the works of Davenant and others who revived British interest in opera after the Restoration, but Italian and Anglo-Italian opera achieved its highest public support in the eighteenth century when artists such as Faustina could be imported at salaries approaching 2,500 pounds in 1726. Large numbers of Italian operas, performed either in their original language or in translation, appeared on the British stage. Their only competition were English pieces "written in the Italian manner" for music by Dr. J. C. Pepusch, Buonocini, and George Frederick Handel, among others, prompting Joseph Addison to comment in the Spectator (#18, 21 March 1711) regarding the fad for works on the order of Arisone (1705), Camilla (1706), Pyrrhus and Demetrius (1708), and Rinaldo and Armira (1711): "There is no question but our great grandchildren will be very curious to sit together like an audience of foreigners in their own country and to hear whole plays acted before them in a tongue which they did not understand."

The "**ballad** opera" or "Newgate pastoral" had been prepared for to some extent, too. Gay was among the most popular **ballad** writers, the populace having been well pleased by his "T'was when the seas were roaring" (1715) and "Sweet William's Farewell" (1720). A successful Christmas pantomine (technically a "**ballad** farce," since it was a one-act entertainment), J. Thurmond's *Harlequin Jack Sheppard; or, The Blossom of Tyburntree* (1724), ran for many nights and not only did it include a tune in thieves; cant, sung by the character Frisky Moll, but Gay himself was a character in the play and it contained his "Newgate's Garland." In addition, Gay would have been familiar with other dramas employing a Newgate setting, such as Brome's *A Joviel Crew*, or *The Merry Beggars* and Christopher Bullock's *Match in Newgate* which was performed three times in 1727.

Two other dramas may also have been direct influences on *The Beggar's Opera*. Charles E. Pearce suggests that *The Prison Breaker*, or the *Adventures of John Sheppard* by an unknown author, served as Gay's model. Although the play remained unperformed until 1728, it was published in 1725 and Pearce feels that there is evidence that Gay had access to a copy of it. Allan Ramsay's *The Gentle Shepherd* is seen by Frank Kidson as a second possible predecessor, for while like *The Prison Breaker* this drama did not reach the state until after *The Beggar's Opera* had been performed, it too was printed in 1725 and Kidson, calling the Scottish writer's work the "first **ballad** opera," argues that Gay would have been acquainted with it.[4] In spite of the vast differences in subject matter and treatment between *The Gentle Shepherd* and *The Beggar's Opera*, Kidson concludes "that Ramsay's work suggested the 'method,' at least, in which Gay's comedy took the form of opera."[5]

When Gay decided on a **burlesque** of the opera form as his medium of expression, he brought all of these traditions together in a way that let him draw upon exactly those **conventions** which suited his need best. Pearce is of the opinion that Gay never meant to **burlesque** the Italian operas then in fashion, but the title of the drama alone would seem to demonstrate that he is mistaken and in the "Introduction" to *The Beggar's Opera* the Beggar calls attention to the fact that he has borrowed "the **similes** that are in your celebrated operas." And the time was certainly ripe for such an endeavor. A prime force in the English theatre for many years, the Italian opera was at the pinnacle of its popularity, attracting large audiences with its excesses and lavish effects (such as turning loose live sparrows in the playhouse). The leading singers commanded high salaries and were of such interest that the petty squabbles between the prima donnas Faustina and Cuzzoni were the talk of the town and the battle between Polly and Lucy would have immediately been seen as a parallel by the audience. Actually, Richard Estcourt's *Prunella*, acted in 1708, was the earliest **burlesque** of the Italian opera, appearing twenty years before *The Beggar's Opera*. Gay, then, was simply weaving all of these popular elements together when he presented his work to the public for the first time on that January evening in 1728, but he did it better than anyone before or since.

SUCCESS

The Beggar's Opera opened at the Theatre Royal in Lincoln's Inn Fields before an audience which included Pope, the Duke of Argyle, and Prime Minister Sir Robert Walpole, the object of much of the play's political **satire**, on January 29, 1728 (often erroneously recorded as 1727). It was an immediate success. Even before the first act concluded, Pope notes that the Duke of Argyle was openly praising the play:

We were all at the first night of it, in great uncertainty of the event; till we were very much encouraged by overhearing the Duke of Argyle, who sat in the next box to us, say, "it will do, - it must do! - I see it in the eyes of them." - This was a good while before the first act was over, and so gave us ease soon; for the duke, (besides his own good taste) has a more particular knack than anyone now living, in discovering the taste of the public. He was quite right in this, as usual; the good nature of the audience appeared stronger and stronger every act, and ended in a clamor of applause.[6]

The Duke was correct, for *The Beggar's Opera* became "by all odds the most popular theatrical work of the eighteenth century,"[7] and has since been judged "an authentic classic and the single most popular musical ever to appear on the English stage."[8]

Including opening night, between January and June 1728 the play ran for 62 performances, 32 of which were consecutive (Pope mistakenly recorded "sixty-three days uninterrupted" in a note to The Dunciad) at a time when a run of four or five nights was considered outstanding. The play was acted 1,081 times by 1800, including eight productions "By Command," 126 "At the Particular Desire of Several Persons of Quality and Distinction," and 172 benefit performances. This unprecedented popularity brought John Rich, the manager of the Theatre Royal, a profit of better than 4,000 pounds (compared to the average theatre manager's "take" of 4,000 pounds for an entire season's productions) and Gay realized seven or eight hundred pounds as the author's share, plus an additional 94 pounds, 10 s., from John Watts and Jacob Tonson, booksellers and printers, for the copyrights to *The Beggar's Opera* and *The Fables* on February 6, 1728. The success of the drama caused London wits to observe that the hit made "Rich gay, and Gay rich."

Besides the fame and money, Gay also accomplished the feat, according to Pope's Dunciad note, of driving "out of England for that season the Italian opera, which had carried all before it for ten years: that idol of the nobility and people which the great critic, Mr. [John] Dennis, by the labors and outcries of a whole life, could not overthrow, was demolished by a single stroke of this gentleman's pen." It also brought an avalanche of imitations, including Gay's own *Polly* (which Walpole ordered the Lord Chamberlain not to license). Thirteen **ballad** operas were authorized the year after Gay's triumph, and the number composed grew each year to a high point of 22 in 1733. Moreover, Thomas Walker, the actor who played the role of Macheath, and Lavinia Fenton, who acted the party of Polly, were subjected to adulation and general acclaim by their admirers. Both were relatively unknown prior to that January evening in 1728, but awoke the next morning to the admiration of an entire country. Walker had difficulty handling the success so suddenly thrust upon him, but Miss Fenton became a "darling" of the public and one of the most famous actresses of her time, even having her portrait painted by William Hogarth. Indeed, she was regarded as "Polly" for the rest of her life.

Interestingly, until the play opened, there was a great deal of doubt that it would survive more than the opening night. Pope claims that when Gay first talked to Swift about his proposed **ballad** opera, "the Doctor did not much like the project,"[9] and Pope himself was sure that the work would make "a great noise," though he was undecided as to whether it would be "of claps or hisses." Gay's friend and patron, the Duke of Queensberry, offered his opinion that, "This is a very odd thing, Gay. I am satisfied that it is either a very good thing, or a very bad thing," and William Congreve remarked that the drama "would either take greatly, or be damned confoundedly."

Once the manuscript was finished, Gay had difficulty in persuading anyone to produce the play. He submitted it first to the manager of London's most reputable playhouse, the Drury Lane Theatre, but the usually theatrically astute Colley Cibber was bothered by the uniqueness of *The Beggar's Opera* and turned instead to *Love in Several Masques*, the maiden effort of young Henry Fielding (the results were disastrous - Fielding was booed off the stage). Gay next turned to Rich, who was similarly hesitant about trying something which did not follow a proven formula for success, but the Duchess of Queensberry intervened on Gay's behalf, agreeing to underwrite any losses which the theatre might suffer. Still, Rich nearly abandoned the play, only to be swayed by the obvious interest of the influential literary circle which surrounded Gay. As it was, Rich produced the drama as cheaply as possible.

Casting turned out to be a problem, too. The well-known actor James Quin was the first choice to play Macheath, but he balked at becoming connected with an endeavor that he felt could not succeed. Following Rich's lead, he finally agreed rather than offend Gay's friends. He attended the first several rehearsals, yet he was not at ease with the role and when his friend Tom Walker was heard singing some of Macheath's songs backstage during one of the rehearsals, Quin declared at once that he would decline the role in Walker's favor, since Walker was obviously better suited to the part.

From that first night, however, the play was on its way and the history of its continuing popularity is astounding. Companies began touring the provinces with productions of *The Beggar's Opera* even before the original Theatre Royal run ended and to Swift's immense delight it soon arrived in Dublin. Its foreign popularity spread quickly. Besides being featured in Scotland, Wales, and Minorca, a British possession, the drama was the first musical to be presented in America (where it became

George Washington's favorite play), when it was produced by the Murray-Kean Company of London. It reached Jamaica in 1733 where disaster overtook the company (within two months the entire company was dead, with the exception of one old man, a woman, and a boy), and it crossed the English Channel as L'Opera du Guex in a translation by A. Hallam which was acted in Paris in 1750 and as Die Strassenrauber it was being performed in Hamburg by 1770.

Since the eighteenth century, *The Beggar's Opera* has been revived on many occasions. It ran for 1,463 performances at the Lyric Theatre in London in 1920 and subsequently appeared in 1922, 1928, 1940 (Sir John Gielgud's production), 1954, 1958 (at the Cambridge Drama Festival), and as late as 1963 when the Royal Shakespeare Company staged it. American revivals include that at the Greenwich Village Theatre Club in 1920 (by 1923 there was a Beggar's Opera Club which limited its membership to those who had seen forty or more performances of the drama), the Interplayers' production in 1950, the 1957–58 New York City Center presentation, and other productions, including a staging at a major New York theatre as recently as the 1972–73 season. In 1953 Sir Laurence Olivier was seen in the role of Macheath in a movie version of the play, and the collaboration of Bertolt Brecht and Kurt Weil on *The Threepenny Opera* in 1928, and *The Beggar's Holiday*, a Broadway musical for which Duke Ellington wrote the score, are among the adaptations of *The Beggar's Opera*, a play which almost died unperformed. Even today some critics trace the influence of *The Beggar's Opera* in such seemingly unrelated pieces as Anthony Burgess' 1962 novel, *A Clockwork Orange* (translated to the movie screen in 1972 by Stanley Kubrick).

NOTES

Eighteenth-Century British Drama

[1] *A Short History of English Drama* (Boston, 1965), p. 129.

[2] See "The Beginning and Significance of Sentimental Comedy," Anglia, 55 (1931), 368–392 and "Sentimental Comedy in the Eighteenth Century," Neophilogues, 18 (1933), 281–289.

[2a] See also "The Genesis of Steele's The Conscious Lovers," Essays Critical and Historical Dedicated to Lily B. Campbell (Berkeley, 1950), pp. 173–182; "Essays on the Theatre from Eighteenth-Century Periodicals," Augustan Reprints (Ann Arbor, 1960), pp. 85–86; and Steele at Drury Lane (Berkeley, 1952).

Introduction To "The Beggar's Opera"

[3] The full title is "Newgate's Garland: Being A New **Ballad**. Shewing How Mr. Jonathan Wild's Throat was cut from Ear to Ear with a Penknife, by Mr. Blake, alias Blueskin, the bold Highwayman, as he stood at his Tryal in the Old-Bailey. 1725."

[4] *The Beggar's Opera: Its Predecessors and Successors* (Cambridge, 1922), pp. 30–33.

[5] Ibid., p. 33.

[6] Recorded in Joseph Spence, Anecdotes (London, 1820), p. 159.

[7] Benjamin W. Griffith, Jr., ed., *The Beggar's Opera* (New York, 1962), p. 19.

[8] C. F. Burgess, ed., *The Beggar's Opera* (New York, 1966), p. viii.

[9] Quoted in Spence, p. 159.

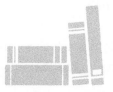

THE BEGGAR'S OPERA

ACT I

....

INTRODUCTION

Before the curtain goes up, two figures emerge onto the stage where they confront one another. One is a very shabbily dressed Beggar, the other a foppishly attired Player. The Beggar says that "If poverty be a title to poetry," he certainly must be a poet, and he admits writing popular songs to make a living. The Player wishes him success and the Beggar goes on to discuss the inspiration of the forthcoming drama, a celebration of the marriage between two ballad-singers which includes operatic **similes** and a pathetic prison scene, but he begs forgiveness if his work is not as artificial as an opera, lacking a recitative, prologue, and epilogue.

ACT I, SCENE 1

The curtain rises to discover Peachum seated at a table in his London house, consulting a large account book. He begins singing "Air I" immediately, which is an account of mankind's roguery, then comments on the theme.

ACT I, SCENE 2

Filch enters with news about Black Moll and he and Peachum enter into a discussion of other members of the gang, leading Peachum to a song on the nature of women. Filch exits.

ACT I, SCENE 3

Peachum returns to his perusal of the account book, reading it aloud - it is a record of the criminal activities of each thief and his contribution to the coffers.

ACT I, SCENE 4

Mrs. Peachum comes in in time to overhear her husband talking about one of her favorites, Bob Booty. Peachum indicates that the man is to be turned in soon, since he represents a danger to the gang because of his fondness for women, and Mrs. Peachum sings "Air III", suggesting that women should not interfere in business matters as they are liable to be swayed by their emotions. The couple considers the topic of murder and Captain Macheath is mentioned as being an excellent provider for the gang. Unfortunately, their daughter Polly is taken with the man and this brings about numerous comments on the subject of marriage, including the singing of another Air by Mrs. Peachum. Marriage is an especially touchy topic in this family, for if Polly marries she holds her parents' fate in her hands, for she would owe allegiance to her husband rather than to them. Peachum runs off stage to terrify his daughter from the idea of marriage by holding up their neighbors to her as examples of married life.

ACT I, SCENE 5

Mrs. Peachum remains behind to sing about fidelity.

ACT I, SCENE 6

Filch returns to display his loot from the previous night's work as a pickpocket. During the conversation he reveals that he knows a secret about Polly and her Captain, and Mrs. Peachum, seeing her husband coming with their daughter, takes Filch to her own room so that he can tell her the secret.

ACT I, SCENE 7   — *Sexas transaction*

Polly enters and talks about the economics of the exchange of love between a man and a woman; then she breaks into a sentimental song about the advisability of keeping the merchandise pure. Peachum warns her that he will have her throat cut if she has gotten married.

ACT I, SCENE 8   *— Inversion*

Mrs. Peachum reenters singing that "Polly is a sad slut!" who has betrayed her mother and father by getting married. Peachum and his wife verbally abuse the girl who has ignored their "lectures of morality" and when Polly refuses to admit her guilt,

Peachum threatens to find out if she really is married by keeping Macheath away from her. Polly sings that she has married so as not to upset her parents, but Mrs. Peachum can only moan, "Then all the hopes of our family are gone for ever and ever!" The three characters continue their discussion of the marriage, causing Mrs. Peachum's swoon when she finds that her daughter married because she was in love. The two women sing a short duet, the mother saying in effect that Polly should have teased, but not given in, with Polly answering that he was so persuasive that no one could have withstood his advances. Peachum says that perhaps they should "all endeavor to make the best of it," and after Polly sings her joy at her mother's forgiveness, he sends her into the other room to attend a customer.

ACT I, SCENE 9

With Polly gone the two Peachum discuss Macheath's financial value, coming to the decision that they must be careful to determine whether or not the Captain is married to anyone else, because when it comes time (possibly "in a Session or two") for Macheath to hang, they do not want all of the money to go for lawyer's fees in a dispute over the legitimacy of her claim on his estate. Peachum sings an Air about the dishonest practices of lawyers.

ACT I, SCENE 10

Polly returns and the conversation centers on how her husband is going to support her. Peachum advises that her best move would be to become a widow as soon as she can by turning Macheath into the law - it is quite simple really, merely a matter of good economics. Polly is upset that they could ask such a thing of her and sings a song asking that they not be so severe in their demands. Mrs. Peachum reminds her that it is her obligation to have Macheath hanged, but Polly still balks, indicating in "Air XIII" that her love would not allow here to survive her husband's death. Peachum threatens her again and Mrs. Peachum sends her away with the admonition, "Away, hussy. Hang your husband, and be dutiful."

ACT I, SCENE 11

As Polly eavesdrops, her parents declare that if she does not have the Captain "peach'd," they will - it is "a case of necessity."

ACT I, SCENE 12

Polly prepares to warn Macheath of his danger.

ACT I, SCENE 13

Before she can leave, however, she encounters Macheath and the couple sing a duet about their love, then talk about fidelity. The highwayman sings that he has been promiscuous, but will love only her from now on and the two engage in another love duet about how they will never part. Polly remembers her parents' plotting, though, and sings about the pain of separation. The act ends as the pair, looking back at each other from opposite doorways, sing a final duet on the subject of losing what one loves most.

THE BEGGAR'S OPERA

ACT II

. . . .

ACT II, SCENE 1

Act II opens in a tavern near Newgate where members of Macheath's gang are gathered. Jemmy Twitcher, Crook-Finger'ds Jack, Wat Dreary, Robin of Bagshot, Nimming Ned, Henry Padington, Matt Of The Mint, and Ben Budge discuss the nature of the criminal life, comparing it to other professions, and concluding that if there is anything about their type of life that differ from anyone else's, it is that they are more honest. A drinking song concludes the scene.

ACT II, SCENE 2

Macheath enters and explains to his followers that he must retreat to their private quarters in order to avoid being arrested on Peachum's evidence, but he warns the gang not to harm Peachum, for he is necessary to keep the business running. The gang sings a rousing tune and goes off to their nightly "duty."

ACT II, SCENE 3

Macheath remains so as to deliver a soliloquy on the attraction women have for him, singing a song about their charms. The Drawer enters to inform him that the "ladies" he has sent for have arrived.

ACT II, SCENE 4

Mrs. Coaxer, Dolly Trull, Mrs. Vixen, Betty Doxy, Jenny Diver, Mrs. Slammekin, Suky Tawdry, and Molly Brazen enter to be greeted warmly by Macheath, who then sings a carpe diem song and they all join in a dance. The women tell Macheath how they use their charms to make money and Jenny sings a couple of melodies for the Captain before she and Suky take his pistols and, while pretending to flirt with him, signal to Peachum and some Constables, who rush in upon him.

ACT II, SCENE 5

Peachum seizes Macheath and the prisoner sings that he will welcome hanging, since then he will find no such traitorous "furies as these." Exit Macheath, guarded by Peachum and the constables.

ACT II, SCENE 6

The women remain behind and quarrel about the reward for betraying the Captain.

ACT II, SCENE 7

Now at Newgate Prison, Captain Macheath is welcomed by the jailor, Lockit, who reminds him that his stay will be much more pleasant if he is willing to bribe ("Garnish") his keepers. Seeing the variety of heavy fetters, Macheath agrees and produces enough money to be able to be handcuffed with the lightest, most comfortable set of chains.

ACT II, SCENE 8

Left alone, Macheath sings about the lack of faithfulness to be found in women, though he amusingly admits that he treats women in the same way.

ACT I, SCENE 9

Lucy enters the cell and abuses the Captain for having made her pregnant, then sings that she is as delighted at seeing him incarcerated as a good housewife would be to find a thieving rat caught in her trap. Macheath asks her why she does not show a little tenderness at finding her husband in this situation. Lucy is amazed that he would claim to be married to her, but he says that they are married "In ev'ry respect but the form." Lucy defies him by singing that he is cruel to take advantage of her and then to boast about it. Macheath counters that they will be married at the "very first opportunity," but again Lucy is prepared for him as she reveals that she knows that he has already married Polly, a charge which the Captain immediately denies, claiming that Polly has jealously invented the marriage herself. He proves his point by singing about women's fondness for their own images in mirrors, a demonstration of their vanity.

ACT II, SCENE 10

Reentering with an account-book, Peachum and Lockit converse about their business affairs, each suggesting that the other has not been exactly honest in their dealings - causing Peachum to observe, "this is the first time my honour was ever call'd in question." The two men actually collar each other and each is prepared to inform on his partner in crime when they realize that they know so much about one another's businesses that they have it in their power to hang each other, so must settle things peacefully in self-defense, for their "mutual interest."

ACT II, SCENE 11

Peachum departs to see to business and Lucy enters, crying. Lockit counsels her "to bear your husband's death like a reasonable woman," while Lucy's song questions her lover's fate. Her father declares that "there is no saving him" and sings that he is really doing her a favor.

ACT II, SCENE 12 — *(clas)*

Returning to Macheath's cell, Lucy reports that she has been unable to soften her father's hard heart and the pair decide that money is the sole solution. Macheath's tune is presented as evidence that this is true.

ACT II, SCENE 13

Into this scene bursts Polly, searching for her husband, much to Macheath's consternation. Polly expresses her suffering in song, only to have her husband disown her in an effort to secure Lucy's help. Lucy refuses Macheath's explanation that Polly is "distracted," and the two women begin berating their mutual husband. Macheath sings that he could be happy with either woman as long as the other were absent, to which Lucy and Polly reply in a funny duet that they have been "Bamboozled!" Macheath again tries to convince Lucy that Polly is either mad or attempting to discredit him so that she can have him to herself if he should escape the gallows. The three continue to argue and insult one another.

ACT II, SCENE 14

Into the round of accusations comes Peachum to fetch his daughter home, but Polly must be dragged, singing, from her lover's cell.

ACT II, SCENE 15

Explaining that he did not dismiss Polly as quickly as he should have because he is "naturally compassionate," Macheath persuades Lucy that he truly loves no one but her. Lucy undertakes to steal her father's keys.

THE BEGGAR'S OPERA

ACT III

....

ACT III, SCENE 1

As Act III opens, Macheath has escaped and Lucy and her father are still at Newgate where Lockit is accusing his daughter of helping the prisoner get away. He soon accepts her guilt in spite of her denials and becomes more interested in a more important subject - how much was she paid for her efforts? Lucy sings that she released the prisoner because of her love, not for monetary reasons, though she is repentant for she now believes that he and Polly are man and wife and she sings about her folly and resentment.

ACT III, SCENE 2

Having sent Lucy away, Lockit theorizes that Peachum is responsible for the chain of events and temporizes that the key to a successful life is cheating your fellow before he can cheat you. And he has a **ballad** ready to demonstrate his contention.

ACT III, SCENE 3

Lockit questions Filch about his master's whereabouts, incidentally commenting on a "great man" who saves the ladies from hanging by helping them become pregnant.

ACT III, SCENE 4

At a gaming-house Macheath, playing cards with Ben Budge and Matt of the Mint, considers the subject of money and the upper class' attitude toward it. This leads his two friends to compare his state with that of the aristocracy. The three make plans to meet later at Marybone.

ACT III, SCENE 5

In Peachum's lock, Peachum and Lockit discuss the disposal of items stolen during King George II's Coronation (1727). Lockit suggests that if Peachum keeps an eye on Polly, he will discover Macheat's location within the next couple of days, though his friend questions the significance of capturing the highwayman if the prison-keeper's daughter will immediately effect his release.

ACT III, SCENE 6

Mrs. Trapes, a lady fond of her liquor, appears for a business conference and innocently reveals the whereabouts of the Captain - he is at Mrs. Coaxer's in Marybone.

ACT III, SCENE 7

Back at Newgate, Lucy is suffering from jealousy, as she prepares to poison her rival, Polly.

ACT III, SCENE 8

The two women greet each other cordially and apologize courteously for their previous antagonistic behavior. After several songs, Lucy departs to fetch the poisoned brandy.

ACT III, SCENE 9

While waiting, Polly discloses to the audience that she suspects Lucy's friendly manners.

ACT III, SCENE 10

Lucy returns with the liquor and Polly is about to drink when she sees Macheath being brought back to prison and drops her glass. Since Macheath is back in Newgate, Lucy is glad that her design has gone awry.

ACT III, SCENE 11

Peachum and Lockit once more escort the prisoner on his way to court to the distress of the women, who both attempt to get him to recognize them as his sole wife. Macheath responds that neither will have to worry long, for he will soon be dead. Polly and Lucy in turn plead with their fathers to spare the Captain's life, but the two men are adamant and will not give in.

ACT III, SCENE 12

Lucy and Polly send Filch to follow the trio and report what happens at the trial. This is followed by "A dance of prisoners in chains, etc."

ACT III, SCENE 13

Macheath, "in a melancholy posture" in the condemned hold, sings a series of tunes relating the history of his downfall. A Jailor announces the arrival of his friends.

ACT III, SCENE 14

Ben Budge and Matt of the Mint hear their leader denounce Jemmy Twitcher for having "peached" him and they agree to honor Macheath's last request-to bring Peachum and Lockit to the gallows.

ACT III, SCENE 15

As Ben and Matt depart, Lucy and Polly enter. Once again the Captain refuses to acknowledge his love for either of them and the play ends as "four wives more" and their children come to see Macheath, who is willingly led off by the sheriff's officers.

ACT III, SCENE 16

After Macheath has been taken away, the Player and the Beggar from the introduction return to the stage where the Player wonders if Macheath is really meant to hang. The Beggar replies that he is, in the interest of "strict poetical justice," but the Player complains that such a conclusion would make the piece a tragedy, which is "manifestly wrong, for an opera must end happily." Taking this objection into consideration, the Beggar grants a reprieve, much to the relief of the Player, who states that this will "comply with the taste of the town." The Beggar ironically sums up the meaning of the drama.

ACT III, SCENE 17

Macheath returns to the problem of two wives and, since he no longer can depend upon the gallows to save him, he chooses Polly, admitting that they were married all along. The play concludes with a dance and a final song.

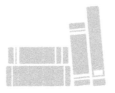

THE BEGGAR'S OPERA

. . . .

PEACHUM

Peachum, the husband of Mrs. Peachum and father of Polly, is a receiver of stolen goods and to this end he has created a large, carefully organized gang of criminals to supply him with merchandise. Besides realizing that he just "protect and encourage cheats, since we live by 'em," Peachum is also quite ready to make a profit by "peaching" on the members of his gang - that is, to earn a reward by giving information to the law. This practice has the added benefit of removing those who might pose a threat to him. As a "businessman," too, Peachum more than anyone else in the play understands that there is little difference between the actions of the lower classes and the actions of the upper classes and he continually recites the drama's major **theme** that "All professions be-rogue one another" and "A rich rogue nowadays is fit company for any gentleman." He is a firm believer, therefore, of doing unto others before they do unto him. Furthermore, his personality is strictly businesslike: he displays little emotion; he is careful in his planning, paying attention to detail and keeping accurate accounts; and he is quick to take advantage of all opportunities.

LOCKIT

Lockit, Lucy's father, is the jailer at Newgate Prison. In this capacity he is also Peachum's partner, a man with whom he shares many of the same desires and philosophies. This is easily seen when Macheath is first brought to prison and Lockit makes it clear that the best way to get along in the world is to "know the custom.... Garnish, Captain, garnish!" On the other hand, he is neither as bright nor as appealing in his character as Peachum.

MACHEATH

Macheath, the gentleman-highwayman, is married to Polly and the lover of Lucy (among others). Indeed, this is the true cause of his downfall, for as he says "I must have women" since "I love the sex" and cannot be contented with just one or two. Both arrests come about because the Captain is unable to deprive himself of female companionship. In other matters, though, he is pragmatic and clearly successful - being the prime example of the observation that it is extremely difficult to distinguish between gentlemen and highwaymen. Like Peachum, he is bright and a good businessman, but unlike his father-in-law, he is loyal to the members of his gang and, when forced by circumstances at the play's end, he admits that he has loved Polly all along. In spite of this he is well-liked by the women of the town who are unhappy to have to turn him in, and his gang respects his leadership and loyalty, a loyalty he returns by being willing to sacrifice himself for the good of the gang. He is a man all too ready, though, to do "the right thing" by the young women he meets.

FILCH

Filch is a young pickpocket who serves in Peachum's gang and whose knowledge of Polly's secret leads to the exposure of her marriage to Captain Macheath.

JEMMY TWITCHER, CROOK-FINGER'D JACK, WAT DREARY, ROBIN OF BAGSHOT, NIMMING NED, HARRY PADINGTON, MAT OF THE MINT, AND BEN BUDGE

Jemmy Twitcher, Crook-Finger'd Jack, Wat Dreary, Robin Of Bagshot, Nimming Ned, Harry Padington, Mat Of The Mint, and Ben Budgeare members of Macheath's gang. A fun-loving group, fond of drinking and wenching, the men consider criminal life a profession which differs little from any other, except that it is more honest in nature. It is through the thoughts of these criminals that Gay comments on "honest" society, drawing open comparisons in their words which are only implied by the reverse parallels he presents elsewhere. Mat of the Mint and Ben Budge seem closer to their Captain than the other members of the gang, for they play cards with him at a gaminghouse (leading to a discussion of the similarities and differences between the underworld and the aristocracy, especially on the subject of money). They also visit the gang leader in his cell, where they agree to work for his revenge by way of bringing about the downfall of Peachum and Lockit. Jemmy Twitcher's actions are less admirable.

MRS. PEACHUM

Mrs. Peachum, Peachum's common-law wife, is Polly's mother. As the wife of a businessman, she takes an interest in her husband's enterprises, though she admits that there are certain areas of the business which women should avoid, such as deciding who should be turned over to the police for hanging, because she feels that "Women indeed are bitter bad judges in these cases, for they are so partial to the brave that they think every man handsome who is going to the camp or the gallows." Mrs. Peachum similarly has very definite ideas about how a proper daughter should act- and one of these ideas is that marriage should be avoided at all cost, for any girl who marries, especially for love rather than for gain, "is a sad slut! nor heeds what we have taught her."

POLLY PEACHUM

Polly Peachum is the young daughter of the Peachums who has married Macheath secretly because of her love for him. Despite her parents' wise advice that she would be better off both economically and by not tying herself to one man if she turns her husband in, Polly's faithfulness to Macheath brings her to warn him of her parents' plans and then to stand by him, even under the most trying circumstances (in the figure of Lucy Lockit) when he is in prison. Though her character is, as James Russell Lowell wrote about James Fenimore Cooper's heroines, "All sappy as maples and flat as a prairie," her perseverance is rewarded in the end.

LUCY LOCKIT

Lucy Lockit is the daughter of the jailer, Lockit, and Polly's rival for she too loves Macheath, and although she has not married the highwayman, Lucy appears to have some prior claim to his affections. By playing on this circumstance, Macheath effects his escape from prison, and by bringing the two girls into a confrontation with one another, Gay manages to satirize a

BRIGHT NOTES STUDY GUIDE

current squabble between the two leading prima donnas of the English opera at the time. While she is driven to an attempted murder, Lucy is really a good girl at heart.

DIANA TRAPES

Diana Trapes buys stolen goods from Peachum to resell in her role of clothier of the women of the underworld. It is while visiting with Peachum and Lockit that this gin-drinking lady betrays Macheath's whereabouts after his escape from Newgate.

JENNY DIVER AND SUKY TAWDRY

Jenny Diver and Suky Tawdry are two of the loose women of the town who enjoy Macheath's attentions and presents. It is they who betray him to Peachum and the constables while he is drinking and sporting with them at the tavern.

MRS. COAXER, DOLLY TRULL, MRS. VIXEN, BETTY DOXY, MRS. SLAMMEKIN, AND MOLLY BRAZEN

Mrs. Coaxer, Dolly Trull, Mrs. Vixen, Betty Doxy, Mrs. Slammekin, and Molly Brazen are, as their names imply, additional women of the lower class rabble who make up the society in which Macheath moves.

DRAWER, CONSTABLES, TURNKEY

Drawer, Constables, Turnkey are minor characters who function simply as technical devices in the plot.

Note

Note: the very names of the characters give an indication not only of the individual so labeled, but also of the nature of the comedy present in *The Beggar's Opera*. Peachum is derived from the verb, to peach, meaning to inform against one's accomplices; Lockit is a suitable name for a jailer; Macheath (son of the heath) fits its bearer, since he is a highwayman and highwaymen often plied their trade on the open heaths surrounding London; Filch derives from the slang expression meaning to steal; similarly, a twitcher is a sneak-thief, and to nim is to steal, a budge is a sneak-thief, and diver is another term applied to pickpockets; Bagshot is the name of one of the disreputable heaths frequented by highwaymen; Paddington and the Mint were notorious districts in London; trapes and slammekin are synonyms for slovenly women; trull and doxy are slang terms applied to prostitutes; and the other names are likewise self-descriptive-dreary, coaxer, vixen, tawdry, and brazen.

THE BEGGAR'S OPERA

. . . .

CRITICAL ANALYSIS OF THE INTRODUCTION

Before the play itself actually begins, two characters appear on stage in front of the curtain, the Beggar, who claims to be the author of the piece and explains his purpose in writing it, and a Player, to whom the explanation is ostensibly directed.

Voicing the common complaint of authors, the Beggar begins by stating that "If poverty be a title to poetry," he can certainly be considered a poet, a claim that Gay himself might well have made. His reference to St. Giles's immediately places his social class for the audience and reenforces his claim of poverty, for St. Giles is both the patron saint of beggars and early eighteenth-century London's equivalent of Skid Row. More importantly, though, the Beggar goes on to say that the play was originally written to celebrate the marriage of two ballad-singers, James Chanter and Moll Lay, whose names immediately suggest the nature of the tunes which will follow. He also makes it clear that the drama is to be a **parody** of Italian operas when he admits that he has "introduced the **similes** that are in your celebrated operas: the Swallow, the Moth, the Bee, the Ship, the Flower, etc." Again, the nature of the names in his catalog indicates that these **similes** will be the objects of his humor and the very fact that he catalogs them makes an implied comment on the artificiality of the form he is about to parody.

Besides, he continues, he has included a "charmingly pathetic" prison scene to appeal to the ladies. Speaking of ladies reminds him of the parts to be played and he boasts that he has "observed such a nice impartiality to our two ladies, it is impossible for either of them to take offense," an obvious **allusion** to the quarrel between the operatic divas, Faustina and Cuzzoni, which was then being carried on and accounts of which were well-known to the audience.

As final evidence that he means to make fun of the Italian opera form, the Beggar notes that he has not made his work "throughout unnatural, like those in vogue," for he has discarded the recitative, prologue, and epilogue. Interestingly, on the opening night this statement caused an amusing incident, since the spectators felt that they were about to be cheated out of the music which usually preceded an opera and they became somewhat restive, causing the director to ask John Hall, who played the part of Lockit, to go out and apologize to the audience before there was any further disturbance. Hall, flustered by the sudden silence which greeted his appearance, blurted out, "Ladies and gentlemen, we-we-beg you'll not call for first and second music, because-because you all know, that there is never any music at all in an opera." Such an admission delighted the house and they responded to the rest of the play in good humor.

CRITICAL ANALYSIS OF ACT I

Scene 1

The curtain rises to discover Peachum seated at a table in his London house, consulting a large account book. He begins singing "Air I" immediately, which is an account of mankind's roguery; then he comments on the theme.

The opening scene is extremely important, for it not only contains a statement of the drama's basic **theme**, it also sets the pattern the play is to follow (the use of songs to make observations or provide evidence for comments), and establishes the light, satiric tone of the work.

Peachum is discovered examining his account books, an action which will soon be found to be characteristic of the man. He immediately breaks into a song which proclaims that "Each neighbor abuses his brother," the main concern of the play. The song also points out the similarity between thieves, priests, lawyers, and so forth, and concludes with the humorous observation that the statesman thinks his trade is as honest as Peachum's.

Peachum then draws a comparison between his employment and that of a lawyer. In addition to providing a statement of Gay's **theme**, the tune and Peachum's subsequent comment are good examples of the humor which is found throughout the drama. First, the satirical words of the song are set to the melody of a popular **ballad**, "Unconstant Roger," that was familiar to all of the audience, and which begins:

An old Woman Cloathed in Grey, Whose Daughter was charming and young, But Chanc'd to be once led astray, By

46

Roger's false flattering Tongue. With whom she too often had been, Abroad in the meadows and Field.

Playing on the audience's expectations, Gay's version contrasts amusingly with its original. (Note: the original versions of many of the songs Gay borrows are recorded in Thomas D'Urfey's collection, *Wit and Mirth, or Pills to Purge Melancholy,* London, 1698, commonly referred to as *Pills* or *Pills to Purge Melancholy,* or in Playford's *The Dancing Master,* various editions, 1650–1728).

Second, another major source of humor lies in the open comparison between characters of Peachum's class and counterparts in the upper classes. Gay is saying that men are dishonest rogues on all levels of society-the only differences being in the manner in which they display their dishonesty and the punishment they receive if caught. Today's student of *The Beggar's Opera* should keep in mind that even while performing the most outlandish acts and treacheries upon one another, the characters in the play continually stress that they are behaving no differently from the most respected members of society and that the fun in the drama comes from hearing the thieves and whores excuse their actions in this way as they reverse the normal moral code of society with their observations that dishonesty is not merely common, it is the best policy.

Perhaps more difficult for the modern student of Gay to follow is the **theme** of political **satire** which is so basic to the plot of *The Beggar's Opera*. To the members of the dramatist's audience, for instance, the line in the song "And the statesman, because he's so great" would have been an overt reference to the Prime Minister, Sir Robert Walpole, who was often sarcastically dubbed the "Great Man." Throughout the play there will be numerous additional references of this nature as the playwright humorously attacks the corruption of the current government (and incurs the wrath of those in power. See the discussions in the "Eighteenth-Century British Drama: Overview" and "The Life and Works of John Gay" sections above for Walpole's reaction to this open criticism and the subsequent dramatic consequences, especially the Licensing Act of 1737). These references add another dimension to the meaning of the drama, for they cause us to interpret both the words and the actions of the characters on more than just a superficial level of what actually takes place on the stage. We must also recognize, therefore, that the author is attributing the moral attitudes not only to his players, but also to those currently holding public offices.

Scene 2

Filch enters with news about Black Moll and he and Peachum enter into a discussion of other members of the gang, leading Peachum to a song on the nature of women. Filch exits.

Filch's opening announcement about Black Moll's trial serves several purposes. First, it makes it clear very quickly what type of people are being dealt with in the play, giving us a better understanding of what Peachum meant in the previous scene when he stated that he lives by protecting and encouraging cheats. Second, it indicates Peachum's power, for Black Moll is looking to him to save her.

Although Peachum points out that Black Moll can "plead her belly" (a reference to the law forbidding the hanging of pregnant women), he does indicate that he will "soften the evidence" for her. This admission has more meaning than its face value of kindness, though, since he is willing to soften the evidence only because Black Moll is useful to him-"the wench is very active and industrious." The **theme** of self-interest as a motivating power is always present in *The Beggar's Opera*.

Filch's further news that Tom Clagg has been found guilty reenforces this **theme** of self-interest, because Peachum has no interest in saving this second gang member, who he feels is a "lazy dog." On the other hand, Betty Sly has been most successful in filling the lock (a warehouse for stolen goods), so she is more valuable in England than in the colonies, to which she would be transported for her crimes if Peachum does not interfere, which, of course, insures that he will. While confessing that saving women is almost a weakness for him, Peachum ironically underscores the economic wisdom behind his practice: it is good business to let the female of the species go free, since she is needed for breeding purposes, and besides, he would receive no reward for her.

Two additional major **themes** are exposed in the exchange between Peachum and Filch. The **theme** of betrayal is instituted when the gang leader expresses his feelings about whether or not he is willing to save the individual gang members and when he insinuates that it is common practice for members to inform upon one another when he says that Betty might live another year, "If none of the gang take her off." Dramatically, this prepares (foreshadows) us for the betrayals centering around Captain Macheath later in the play. In addition, the casual comment that "there is nothing to be got by the death of women-except our wives," demonstrates the attitude toward marriage held by the characters in the drama and similarly prepares us for the reactions of Polly's mother and father to the announcement about her forthcoming marriage to Macheath. This in turn provides us with an understanding of how the parents can so readily think of betrayal of the Captain as an answer to their objections. After all, Polly's decision to marry amounts to a betrayal of their reversed moral code!

The scene closes with Peachum's ironic referral to his friends in Newgate, the notorious London prison. His use of the word friend is amusing in light of what he has just admitted about what he views as the most important elements in his relationships with other people.

Scene 3

Peachum returns to his perusal of the accounts book, reading it a loud-it is a record of the criminal activities of each thief and his contribution to the coffers.

In his soliloquy Peachum continues to expand the **theme** of self-interest, as he makes his preparations for when to betray various gang members-according to their value of his coffers. He will not expose Crook-finger'd Jack at the "next Sessions," the quarterly standing of the criminal court, since Jack is performing well as a high-wayman ("upon the road"), but Slippery Sam is a "villain" to be removed from the gang because he wants to leave the organization and go straight. Once again Gay introduces "Bob" Walpole's name into the dialogue when Peachum mentions Robin of Bagshot, "alias Gorgon, alias Bluff Bob, alias Carbuncle, alias Bob Booty"-all recognizable references to the Prime Minister. There is further humor in the naming of Robin of Bagshot, since Bagshot Heath was a favorite haunt outside London where robbers lurked, and the audience would be quick to equate Bagshot Heath with the Houses of Parliament.

Scene 4

Mrs. Peachum comes in in time to overhear her husband talking about one of her favorites, Bob Booty. Peachum indicates that the man is to be turned in soon, since he represents a danger to the gang because of his fondness for women, and Mrs. Peachum sings "Air III", suggesting that women should not interfere in business matters as they are liable to be swayed by their emotions. The couple considers the topic of murder and Captain Macheath is mentioned as being an excellent provider for the gang. Unfortunately, their daughter Polly is taken with the man and this brings about numerous comments on the subject of marriage, including the singing of another air by Mrs. Peachum. Marriage is an especially touchy topic in this family, for if Polly marries she holds her parents' fate in her hands, for she would owe allegiance to her husband, rather than to them. Peachum runs off stage to terrify his daughter from the idea of marriage by holding up their neighbors to her as examples of married life.

Mrs. Peachum's entrance at this point is amusing because of her noting that Bob Booty is a favorite "customer" of hers. Walpole surely would not have been happy to see himself accused of acquaintance with this kind of woman.

Mrs. Peachum's interest in Bob Booty's fate would be touching, in spite of her husband's reminder that the forty-pound reward will be lost to them if they do not turn him in before one of his other friends does, except that her expression of concern is followed by a confession that women are naturally soft-hearted and emotional, especially about men going into the military ("camp") or soon to be hanged. Women, then, are portrayed as so subject to their emotions that they are attracted to a man not for what he is, but for the circumstances which surround him. This is a double **irony**, first placing Walpole in such a category, then indicating that there is not necessarily even anything about him personally which might contribute to the attraction; it is only his position.

By stressing the emotional nature of women and their consequent weakness in "Air III", Mrs. Peachum lays the foundation for her contention later in the scene that Polly, as a girl in love, will be subject to her emotions. Ironically, though Mrs. Peachum's evidence of weakness and an "overscrupulous conscience" regarding murder shows that there is little to differentiate between her morals and ethics and those of her husband. Mr. Peachum finds murder a trivial subject, not worth "whimpering" about: "No gentleman is ever look'd upon the worse for killing a man in his own defense and if business cannot be carried on without it, what would you have a gentleman do?" That there is no moral equivalence between the two reasons for murder (i.e., self defense and business) does not seem to occur to Peachum. And, anyway, "Murder is as fashionable a crime as a man can be guilty of"-a fine indictment of society, if true.

The mention of Captain Macheath is a good example of how Gay utilizes the technique of reversal to make his points. The Captain is judged a fine gentleman by Mrs. Peachum, in spite of the fact that the bank has stopped payment on his notes, because he is "cheerful" and "agreeable." As criteria for judgment, these two attributes are a bit lacking in depth. What Gay is implying, though, is that it is exactly this type of superficial criteria by which the upper classes are judged. As Peachum says, there are class distinctions, as evidenced by the fact that one must be trained in idleness from youth in the manner of the rich if one wants to be successful at places like Marybone, an infamous gambling resort near London which Macheath frequents. There is a parallel between the upper and lower classes present in the reference to a "Temple coffee-house," however, the Temple being the section of London in which the Inns of Court (law schools) are located.

Mrs. Peachum has been interested in the possibility of Macheath's becoming a successful gambler, she now reveals, because she thinks that their daughter, Polly and the gamester are fond of each other. Peachum ironically responds that it would be madness for Polly to marry the man, but his wife reminds him that passion overcomes logic in women in love. Her air, which carries love/fire **imagery**, also involves humor by virtue of being sung from the girl's point of view (the girl might lose her virginity because of her emotions), a reversal of the original song ("Why is your faithful slave disdain'd") in which the young man unsuccessfully begs for his love's favors. Such an explanation does little to soothe Peachum, who expresses the reason for his fear that Polly will marry. The key to his reasoning is his use of the word "prudent." He does not really care what Polly does, except it she marries. For then they will never be safe, because they will be vulnerable to the husband who will know their secrets through Polly and will, therefore, have them in his power. It is this realization which motivates all of the actions of Mr. and Mrs. Peachum for the rest of the play.

Before the scene closes, Gay returns to two of his favorite themes briefly. Class distinctions are again evident when the comparison is drawn between court ladies, who display superficiality and lack of emotion by being able to dispassionately be involved with a dozen young fellows simultaneously, and Polly, who is capable of burning with passion. Marriage is touched on, too, when Peachum goes to warn his daughter that she is facing ruin, a contention he will prove by terrifying her with the example of their neighbors.

There is also an interesting use of language in Peachum's tirade against his daughter's marriage, when he suggests that she should not make herself a "property." The employment of a business term is characteristic of Peachum, of course, but it may also reflect the middle-class attitude toward marriage which was developing at this time, and several of the characters, including Polly herself, will use economic terms in relation to marriage later in *The Beggar's Opera*.

Scene 5

Mrs. Peachum remains behind to sing about fidelity. In "Air V" Mrs. Peachum expresses the woman's point of view regarding marriage and faithfulness in marriage-it's no big deal. As a matter of fact, Mrs. Peachum feels that a married woman is likely to be even more appealing because she belongs to someone else.

Scene 6

Filch returns to display his loot from the previous night's work as a pickpocket. During the conversation, he reveals that he knows a secret about Polly and her Captain, and Mrs. Peachum, seeing her husband coming with their daughter, takes Filch to her own room so that he can tell her the secret.

Scene 6 does little to advance either the plot or the thematic elements of the play and seems primarily to allow Polly to appear for the first time in the following scene at the same time that her mother discovers the nature of her secret.

Mrs. Peachum and Filch discuss business momentarily, then Mrs. Peachum provides an attack on the British educational system when she suggests that Filch should go to school at Marybone or Hockley in the Hole (where bear-baiting and other such events took place). Next, she tells Filch what his important subjects of study should be-all dealing with crime, naturally. Using this as a point of departure, she informs her pupil that he should never tell her a lie and, having established this point, she gets to the question she has been leading up to all the time: does Filch know if there is anything between Polly and Captain Macheath? Filch admits that he does know what is happening.

Scene 7

Polly enters and talks about the economics of the exchange of love between a man and a woman; then she breaks into a sentimental song about the advisability of keeping the merchandise pure. Peachum warns her that he will have her throat cut if she has gotten married.

Polly, unconsciously mocking the upper class, assures her father that she know how to be mercenary, even though she has never been at court. This knowledge is inherent in the nature of women. By putting these words in his heroine's mouth, Gay manages to make fun of women in general, upper class women, and Polly in particular, as he indicates that women are not very admirable and that Polly does not realize that she is incriminating herself through her admission.

Polly enters into the economic spirit that her father displayed earlier when she talks about love as a bargain: a girl trades "some trifling liberties" for material merchandise in the form of a watch and other trinkets. Peachum approves of this approach to the relations between men and women, but warns her that he will cut her throat if she has "play'd the fool" and been so immoral as to get married.

Scene 8

Mrs. Peachum reenters singing that "Polly is a sad slut!" who has betrayed her mother and father by getting married. Peachum and his wife verbally abuse the girl who has ignored their "lectures of morality" and when Polly refuses to admit her guilt, Peachum threatens to find out if she really is married by keeping Macheath away from her. Polly sings that she has married so as not to upset her parents, but Mrs. Peachum can only moan, "Then all the hopes of our family are gone for ever and ever!" The three characters continue their discussion of the marriage, causing Mrs. Peachum's swoon when she finds that her daughter married because she was in love. The two women sing a short duet, the mother saying in effect that Polly should have teased, but not given in, with Polly answering that he was so persuasive that no one could have withstood his advances. Peachum says that perhaps they should "all endeavor to make the best of it," and after Polly sings her joy at her mother's forgiveness, he sends her into the other room to attend to a customer.

Scene 8 is one of the finest examples in *The Beggar's Opera* of Gay's technique at work, for the author employs inversion and plays on the audience's expectations and familiarity with currently popular melodramas to create humor. Mrs. Peachum's entering air (sung to the tune of "Oh London is a fine town," an extremely popular and merry song, the recognition of which would have delighted the playgoers) combines the inversion and melodramatic elements in its first line, as she claims, like many a mother of a beautiful daughter in the dramas of the period, that Polly does not heed what her parents have taught her and is a "sad slut!" But she is a sad slut for getting married, not for giving in to her lover's demands before the wedding! Mrs. Peachum continues in this vein, reversing normal morality by reviling her daughter ("baggage ... hussy ... inconsiderate jade") for making such a fatal mistake.

Peachum's immediate reaction is that the Captain must have married Polly in expectation of getting some of her fortune, since some men will risk "anything" for money. He then reminds his daughter that he and his wife could never have lived together so happily if they had been married.

Mrs. Peachum returns to the fray with more samples of reversal, wondering how Polly intends to support her husband and equating highwaymen and lords (one of the dramatist's major points, of course) by claiming that marrying one is just as bad as marrying the other.

The rest of the scene is involved with Mr. and Mrs. Peachum's agonized realization that things are getting "worse and worse," that Polly is not so well-bred as they thought, since she can so easily allow herself to be married (instead of merely seduced). Furthermore, she does not demonstrate the practicality of Mrs. Peachum, who admits that while the sex is frail, women should realize that they are in a strong bargaining position only so long as they are careful (that is, remain virgins) and that once they are "frail," they lose their advantage and so should make the best of it the first time. Indeed, Polly is so naive that she thinks that her troubles are over when her mother and father display a desire for reconciliation-regardless of her mother's caveat that with marriage her troubles are just now beginning, another disparaging comment about the institution of wedlock.

The entire scene, mother and father berating the daughter who is divided between her familial duties and the demands of her heart, is a broad **parody** of a stock eighteenth-century melodramatic stage convention-the parents' insistence on an arranged marriage of convenience rather than a marriage of love. The contrast with the seriously sentimental comedies of the time is hilarious.

The contrast in attitudes contained in the words of "Air IX", in which the mother regrets that her daughter did not toy with and kiss her man, and the original version of the song, "Oh Jenny, oh Jenny, where hast thou been?" (also known as "The Willoghby Whim" and as "May Fair"), in which a young maiden is upbraided for having strayed, epitomizes the entire exchange.

Scene 9

With Polly gone, the two Peachums discuss Macheath's financial value, coming to the decision that they must be careful to determine whether or not the Captain is married to anyone else, because when it comes time (possibly "in a Session or two') for Macheath to hang, they do not want all of the money to go for lawyer's fees in a dispute over the legitimacy of her claim on his estate. Peachum sings an air about the dishonest practices of lawyers.

Mr. and Mrs. Peachum's discussion on the present state of affairs continues to link the upper classes with immorality ("why the very best families have excus'd and huddled up a frailty of that sort"), to lambast marriage ("a blemish"), and to recognize the all powerful quality of money, a "true fuller's earth for reputations" (fuller's earth is a claylike substance used as an agent for filtering out impurities). Peachum also repeats his earlier contention that lawyers are the worst thieves of all.

Scene 10

Polly returns and the conversation centers on how her husband is going to support her. Peachum advises that her best move would be to become a widow as soon as she can by turning Macheath into the law-it is quite simple, really, merely a matter of good economics. Polly is upset that they could ask such a thing of her and sings a song asking that they not be so severe in their demands. Mrs. Peachum reminds her that it is her obligation to have Macheath hanged, but Polly still balks, indicating in "Air XIII" that her love would not allow her to survive her husband's death. Peachum threatens her again and Mrs. Peachum sends her away with the admonition, "Away, hussy. Hang your husband, and be dutiful."

Marriage is again a main topic of conversation in this scene, with Peachum informing us that the whole reason for marriage is for the wife to benefit through her husband's death. It is reasonable, therefore, to expect his daughter to "peach" on her husband at the earliest opportunity. He also offers an easy rationalization, that Macheath would rather be turned in by his own family than by strangers, and that it is purely a matter of business, anyway, and should be understood as such. After all, everyone understands that while it is Macheath's business to rob, so is it their employment to "take" robbers. Thus there can be no malice intended.

The remainder of the scene concerns Polly and Mrs. Peachum in a debate over duty. Polly states that she cannot murder the man she loves, but her mother insists that it is her duty to do so. For Mrs. Peachum, obviously, duty is that which has to do with saving herself and her family, not a wife's duty to her husband. Finally, Mrs. Peachum is of the opinion that Polly's foolishness in believing in love must stem from her reading "Those cursed play-books."

Scene 11

As Polly eavesdrops, her parents declare that if she does not have the Captain "peach'd," they will-it is "a case of necessity." There is never any doubt in the parents' minds that they must rid themselves of the potential danger represented by Macheath's control of their daughter. Peachum hesitates momentarily, not because he is squeamish about disposing of the Captain, but because he is sorry to have to personally take a hand in the death of a man who has been so good a provider for the gang (everything would be all right, if only they could have convinced Polly to do it). Realizing that his own life is in danger, though, in one of the key speeches of the play, Peachum very firmly asserts that it must be done when he sums up the primary **theme** with his statement, "Then, indeed, we must comply with the customs of the world, and make gratitude give way to interest".

Scene 12

Polly prepares to warn Macheath of his danger. Scene 12 is another parody of eighteenth-century drama. Actually, Polly's wretched circumstances could be those of Amanda in Colley Cibber's sentimental comedy *Love's Last Shift* (1696), or those, of any of her dramatic sisters. It is amusing, too, that her feelings for her sweetheart, whom she already sees in the cart, parallel the description delivered in Scene 4 by Mrs. Peachum when she comments on the weakness of women for men about to be hanged (the Jack Ketch referred to was a seventeenth-century hangman whose name had become generic by the time *The Beggar's Opera* was written).

Scene 13

Before she can leave, however, she encounters Macheath and the couple sing a duet about their love, then talk about fidelity. The highwayman sings that he has been promiscuous, but will love only her from now on and the two engage in another love duet about how they will never part. Polly remembers her parents' plotting, though, and sings about the pain of separation. The act ends as the pair, looking back at each other from opposite doorways, sing a final duet on the subject of losing what one loves most.

Macheath appears for the first time in the play in another stock eighteenth-century scene which is reduced to humor by the obvious **parody** and unfitting **imagery** present. His opening song, for instance, contains a funny play on words. "Pretty parrot say ... " has become "Pretty Polly, say ..., " which is a nice touch, since Polly is a common name for parrots, and Polly seems to be little more than a parrot, naively repeating meaningless platitudes about love learned from romances she has read (as her mother suspected).

There is both **irony** and humor in the intense declarations of love by the two lovers (and perhaps a glancing reference to the city versus country theme then prevalent in literature in Macheath's choice of **allusions** to women with looking-glasses and at quadrilles). Humorously, in spite of their protestations of love, the two part immediately after stating that nothing could keep them apart. And Macheath, regardless of his vow never to be torn from Polly, like Peachum two scenes previously, when it becomes a practical matter of escaping from prison in Act II, will quickly let discretion become the better part of fidelity and soon accept Lucy's advances.

Many of the meetings between Polly and Captain Macheath have a tone reminiscent of the confrontations between Romeo and Juliet in Shakespeare's play. Even some of their lines seem to echo lines from Romeo and Juliet: "One kiss and then-one kiss-begone-farewell."

CRITICAL ANALYSIS OF ACT II

Scene 1

Act II opens in a tavern near Newgate where members of Macheath's gang are gathered. Jemmy Twitcher, Crook-Finger'd Jack, Wat Dreary, Robin Of Bagshot, Nimming Ned, Henry Padington, Matt Of The Mint, and Ben Budge discuss the nature of the criminal life, comparing it to other professions, and concluding that if there is anything about their type of life that differs from anyone else's, it is that they are more honest. A drinking song concludes the scene.

In their discussion of the life of the criminal classes, the members of the gang reiterate Gay's main point through the question raised by Jimmy Twitcher: "Why are the laws levell'd at us? are we more dishonest than the rest of mankind?" The answer to this rhetorical question is clearly "No," in the dramatist's opinion.

The discussion also leads to an **exposition** of the advantages and rights of the lower class. Crook-Finger'd Jack, Wat Dreary, Robin Of Bagshot, Nimming Ned, and Henry Padington all advance reasons for seeing their life and companionship as being agreeable; even superior to that of a gang of courtiers, offers Matt Of The Mint. It is an Arcadian, Robin Hood-and-his-Merry Men picture that they paint, for "every man hath a right to enjoy life," and, as Matt of the Mint points out, avarice is hateful and all they are doing is making their own lives more agreeable by taking from avaricious people things which they would not know how to use correctly anyway. The argument that each social class is represented in literature as being better than all other social classes in some way has been studied by William Empson in *Some Versions of the Pastoral* (New York, 1938), which examines *The Beggar's Opera* as one of the examples. The dialogue between the members of the gang seems to support Empson's claims.

Scene 2

Macheath enters and explains to his followers that he must retreat to their private quarters in order to avoid being arrested on Peachum's evidence, but he warns the gang not to harm Peachum, for he is necessary to keep the business running. The gang sings a rousing tune and goes off to their nightly "duty."

Scene 2 serves to advance the plot and to expose Macheath's attitude toward two subjects, his realization of Peachum's value to the gang and his dispute with his father-in-law. His concern for the gang's welfare prohibits their disposing of Peachum, for, as Macheath states, he is "a man that is useful to us ... Business cannot go on without him." Practical economics takes precedence over personal desires even here. And Macheath is not overly worried by the disagreement with Polly's family anyhow. He sees it as only a "slight difference" which will be reconciled in a week or so. Perhaps he can view the situation so lightly because of his attitude toward Polly and women as a whole which is expressed in the following two scenes.

Some critics have seen a political analogy in the relationship between Macheath, Peachum, and the members of the gang. Macheath is the acknowledged ruler of the organization, like King George II, but it is Peachum, like Walpole, who controls the treasury and, thus, is the real power.

The scene is concluded with a comic march. Taken from Handel's 1711 opera, *Rinaldo and Armida*, the air is amusingly presented when sung by the gang as an unlikely chorus-the incongruity of a collection of criminals singing a heroic military piece is highlighted by them singing it as a chorus-and further humor derives from the contrast between the heroism of the original and the sentiments of Gay's song, which notes that the bandits are like alchemists, turning the lead of their pistol balls into gold removed from traveler's purses.

Scene 3

Macheath remains so as to deliver a soliloquy on the attraction women have for him, singing a song about their charms. The Drawer enters to inform him that the "ladies" he has sent for have arrived.

Macheath, who a mere three scenes before was seen vowing eternal faithfulness to his one true love, Polly, is now seen in a different light, proving that no one's words can be taken at face value. "I love the sex," he admits, claiming that he can never be content with just one woman. He must have women, for they are the elixer of life for him: "nothing unbends the mind like them." The **irony** is that it is women who constantly prove Macheath's downfall, as they continually betray him, the first instance of this coming in the following scene.

Macheath also includes the play-goers in the **satire** when he announces that Drury Lane, the site of the London theatres, would be uninhabited if he and other "gentlemen" like himself did not attract "free-hearted ladies" (i.e., prostitutes) to the area.

Scene 4

Mrs. Coaxer, Doll, Trull, Mrs. Vixen, Betty Doxy, Jenny Diver, Mrs. Slammekin, Suky Tawdry, and Molly Brazen enter to be greeted warmly by Macheath, who then sings a carpe diem song and they all join in a dance. The women tell Macheath how they use their charms to make money. Jenny sings a couple of melodies for the Captain before she and Suky take his pistols and, pretending to flirt with him, signal to Peachum and some Constables, who rush in upon him.

The first actual betrayal scene of *The Beggar's Opera*, Scene 4 begins innocently. Macheath compliments all of the women from Hockley, Vinegar Yard, and Lewkner's Lane, three disreputable London districts, whom he has sent for and proves his contention that he thrives on the attentions of numerous women. The entire situation is made even more ludicrous by Macheath's usage of the opening line spoken by Duke Orsino in Shakespeare's play, *Twelfth Night*, for "If music be the food of love, play on" in Shakespeare's comedy sets the background for a drama which is concerned with the subject of love, while Macheath is obviously not talking about love at all under these circumstances.

The dance and "Air XXII" add to the humor of the scene, since the song is a traditional argument to "Gather ye rosebuds while ye may," for "Time's on the wing" and no one can eat, drink, and be merry when they are old, or worse yet, dead, but the song is set to the tune of a cotillion, an elaborate and very formal social dance.

The upper classes and the lower classes are both mocked by Macheath when he refers to the drinking problem of some of the women, who like ladies of quality are never without the "cholic" for an excuse to imbibe gin - bringing to mind the vivid pointings by Gay's contemporary, William Hogarth, portraying the evils of gin drinking in London's poor sections.

The women entertain Macheath with explanations of how they ply their trades, using sex as a distraction when shoplifting, and so forth, and they are soon involved in exchanging insults, which Macheath labels compliments. They also discuss who make the best "customers" when they employ sex as sex.

As the scene progresses, Macheath finds that Jenny Diver is "not so fond of [him] ... as [she] use to be," an ironically perceptive statement in view of the fact that a few moments later she playfully takes possession of his pistols and in a scene parodying the betrayal at Christ's Last Supper, she kisses the Captain as a sign for the constables, led by Peachum, to rush in to seize Macheath as he drinks his wine.

Scene 5

Peachum seizes Macheath and the prisoner sings that he will welcome hanging, since he will find no such traitorous "furies as these" then. Exit Macheath, guarded by Peachum and the constables.

Having been seized by Peachum, Macheath hears his captor compare him to the "greatest heroes" who, like himself, have been ruined by women. In "Air XXV" the Captain ironically claims that at least in prison he will not suffer from his acquaintance with "furies" like these - forgetting for the moment that the betrayed Lucy, daughter of the jailor, will be waiting for him there.

Scene 6

The women remain behind and quarrel about the reward for betraying the Captain. The women whom Macheath has treated so well are not upset about the duplicity practiced by two of their members which resulted in the capture of a friend, or even about the capture of that friend, but they are upset that they have not been included in the reward, part of Gay's continuing commentary on friendship.

Scene 7

Now at Newgate Prison, Captain Macheath is welcomed by the jailor, Lockit, who reminds him that his stay will be much more pleasant if he is willing to bribe ("Garnish") his keepers. Seeing the variety of heavy fetters, Macheath agrees and produces enough money to be able to be handcuffed with the lightest, most comfortable set of chains.

Lockit (a fitting name for a jailor) welcomes the Captain, calling him noble and a gentleman, two words which emphasize his demand for a bribe. As Macheath observes, only a rich man can be comfortable in prison and die "like a gentleman" when prices are so high, though the existence of a "genteely" made pair of fetters, which fit as easily as gloves, indicates that gentlemen are not strangers to Newgate. The practice of treating prisoners according to the amount they pay the keeper was common.

Scene 8

Left alone, Macheath sings about the lack of faithfulness to be found in women, though he amusingly admits that he treats women the same way. Macheath's singing that "He that tastes woman, ruin meets" loses its significance as a complaint somewhat when it is immediately followed by his admission that he is about to face the wrath of a young lady to whom he has promised marriage - but then, "What signifies a promise to a woman?" Macheath's real concern is that his stay in the custody of her father will be less pleasant due to his indiscretion. Like the women who betrayed him at the tavern, Macheath is not concerned with the person mistreated, only with his own comfort.

Scene 9

Lucy enters the cell and abuses the Captain for having made her pregnant; then she sings that she is as delighted at seeing him incarcerated as a good housewife would be to find a thieving rat caught in her trap. Macheath asks her why she does not show a little tenderness at finding her husband in this situation. Lucy is amazed that he would claim to be married to her, but he says that they are married "In ev'ry respect but the form." Lucy defies him by singing that he is cruel to take advantage of her and then to boast about it. Macheath counters that they will be married at the "very first opportunity," but again Lucy is prepared for him as she reveals that she knows he has already married Polly, a charge which the Captain immediately denies, claiming Polly has jealously invented the marriage herself. He proves his point by singing about women's fondness for their own images in mirrors, a demonstration of their vanity.

Macheath's character is well presented in Scene 9. In order to save himself he is willing to do anything, no matter how outrageous - and he gets away with it! He has no scruples about lying to Lucy, making the surprising announcement that he is her husband, then being quick enough to invent a story which convinces her that he is "a man of honour" and that his word "is as good as his bond." He admits toying with Polly, after the manner of all gentlemen but his offer of marriage with full knowledge of the consequences of bigamy (which is funny in view of subsequent revelations regarding several other wives) together with his song about the nature of women (which Lucy unquestioningly accepts as valid) persuades Lucy that he has been telling her the truth. One might feel that the Captain is justified in his actions because of the severity of his situation, that he is right to do anything which might save him, yet his attitude suggests that he is not really worried about his condition, for he launches into his offense quite easily and effortlessly, thus effectively staunching Lucy's tirade by turning her to the defensive. This method seems to be his normal way of handling himself.

"Air XXVIII", "How cruel are the traytors," shows that Gay played no favorites when borrowing tunes. The original version of this **ballad** (with music attributed to Handel) was originally contained in Gay's earlier play, *The What D'ye Call It* (1715) as "T'was when the sea was roaring." In the original the subject revolves around the loss of a loved one and the subsequent death of the woman who pines away in agony for her missing lover, a far cry from the topic of cheating in love explored in the revision.

Scene 10

Reentering with an account-book, Peachum and Lockit converse about their business affairs, each suggesting that the other has not been exactly honest in their dealings-causing Peachum to observe, "this is the first time my honour was ever call'd in question." The two men actually collar each other and each is prepared to inform on his partner in crime when they realize that they know so much about one another's businesses that they have it in their power to hang each other. So they must settle things peacefully in self-defense, for their "mutual interest."

The main point of this scene seems to be a reiteration of the concept that the characters in *The Beggar's Opera* are rogues-and that they are, therefore, no different from anybody else. After complaining that the government is in arrears on payments of rewards owed them for informing on their compatriots, Peachum and Lockit further the equation between statesmen and the criminal classes by noting that their reputable profession depends on their encouraging those who "betray their friends" like "great statesmen." The parallel between politicians and these two crooks is based on practical hypocrisy, too, as indicated when Peachum informs Lockit that they should not quarrel: "T'is our mutual interest; 'tis for the interest of the world we should agree." The "interest of the world" being used as the reason for doing something which is really of a personal nature is a common failing among politicians, and Gay is not lax in demonstrating this through his parallel. After all, the practice of saving the lives of their acquaintances without being paid for it is not expected of their "betters," so why should it be expected of them, Peachum wonders. And the air, "When you censure the age," actually is forcasting Walpole's reaction when it notes that each courtier immediately becomes defensive when confronted with the mention of vice or bribery, probably because the charge hits too close to home.

Having established the equation between these criminal characters and statesmen, Gay underscores their corruption through their arguing. This is further enforced during the quarrel by their revealing through mutual charges how each has betrayed friends on one occasion or another. Indeed, Lockit humorously becomes so offended by his companion's accusations that he exclaims, "this is the first time my honour was ever call'd into question"-not that there was ever a question of honor involved with these two. The paraphrase from Shakespeare's *Othello* is especially amusing since it is a complete reversal of the sentiment contained in the original: "Who steals my purse steals trash; 'tis something, nothing;/ 'Twas mine,'tis his, and has been slave to thousands;/ But he that filches from me my good name/ Robs me of that which not enriches him,/ And makes me poor indeed."

Scene 11

Peachum departs to see to business and Lucy enters, crying. Lockit counsels her "to bear your husband's death like a reasonable woman," while Lucy's song questions her lover's fate. Her father declares "there is no saving him" and sings that he is really doing her a favor.

A certain sense of continuity comes from this scene between Lucy and her father, for it parallels in both reactions and ideas the earlier confrontations between Polly and her parents. There is a lack of sympathy-no woman would marry without the hope of her husband's death and her best profit comes from her husband's death, according to the parents in *The Beggar's Opera*. The daughters' reactions are the same, too. Like Polly before her, Lucy admits that as a woman she is frail in her emotions, especially in regard to love, and, moreover, she feels her responsibility to the man she loves, as opposed to her father.

Scene 12

Returning to Macheath's cell, Lucy reports that she has been unable to soften her father's hard heart and the pair decide that money is the sole solution. Macheath's tune is presented as evidence that this is true. Scene 12 merely repeats the contention that money is all-powerful, that anything, anywhere, can be accomplished if enough money is applied. The willingness of Lucy to work for her lover's escape because of his professed love for her suggests that this may have been part of the motivation behind the Captain's actions from the very beginning.

Scene 13

Into this scene bursts Polly, searching for her husband, much to Macheath's consternation. Polly expresses her suffering in song, only to have her husband disown her in an effort to secure Lucy's help. Lucy refuses Macheath's explanation that Polly is "distracted," and the two women begin berating their mutual husband. Macheath sings that he could be happy with either woman as long as the other were absent, to which Lucy and

Polly reply in a funny duet that they have been "Bamboozled!" Macheath again tries to convince Lucy that Polly is either mad or attempting to discredit him so that she can have him to herself, if he should escape the gallows. The three continue to argue and insult one another.

One of the funniest sequences in the drama, Scene 13 brings the three main characters together in a confrontation which obviously is meant as a spoof of conventional operatic scenes. From Polly's humorous interruption through "Air XXXVI", a clear mocking of the Italian operatic recitative tradition, to the final exchange between the two women, Gay is having fun with his **parody** of the operatic form and the contemporary quarrel between London's two leading prima donnas, Faustina and Cuzzoni (see above, the "Background to *The Beggar's Opera*", for an account of this famous tiff).

Macheath's discomfiture is amusing too. In the face of Polly's protestations that no force can tear her from him, reminding us of their similar promises at the end of Act I, he must disown her in order to further his scheme to get Lucy to help him escape. His motivation is clear when he protests in an aside that he is an "unfortunate rascal" and must "disown" her. A problem arises, though, because Lucy is now convinced that she has been doubly wronged-for loving him, in the first place, and for allowing him to persuade her that he still cares, in the second place. Where women were blamed for deceiving men in the previous scenes, now Lucy proclaims the lying nature of men. Again, as throughout the play, Gay seems to be saying that such is the nature of humankind and the world-as declared in the opening air of *The Beggar's Opera*, everyone cheats everyone else in this life.

"Air XXXVII" is another tune originally intended for a **ballad** by Gay, "Sweet William's Farewell to Black-Ey'd Susan" (1720), which tells the story of a sailor's taking his farewell.

Scene 14

Into the round of accusations comes Peachum to fetch his daughter home. The sight of Peachum dragging off Polly while she sings her love for Macheath is one of the highlights of the play, a humorous exaggeration of a stock operatic situation.

Scene 15

Explaining that he did not dismiss Polly as quickly as he should have because he is "naturally compassionate," Macheath persuades Lucy that he truly loves no one but her. She is easily won over, and as a proof of her love will attempt to take her father's keys from him (a simple task, since the jailor is drunk in bed after drinking with the prisoners). She suspects that Polly may have more of a hold on Macheath than he admits to (he wins her confidence by arguing that Polly's father would not have taken him if there were anything between him and Polly), but lets her love overcome her suspicions in spite of Macheath's explanation of why she cannot accompany him.

CRITICAL ANALYSIS OF ACT III

Scene 1

As Act III opens, Macheath has escaped and Lucy and her father are still at Newgate where Lockit is accusing his daughter of helping the prisoner get away. He soon accepts her guilt in spite of her denials and becomes more interested in a more important subject-how much was she paid for her efforts. Lucy sings that she released the prisoner because of her love, not for monetary reasons, though she is repentant, for she now believes that he and Polly are man and wife. She sings about her folly and resentment.

As we have come to expect, money is the main motivating force evidenced in this scene. Lockit can forgive his daughter for her duplicity, provided she does not "cheat" him by withholding any profit she made from the Captain's escape.

Lucy, too, is caught up in the economic aspects of life. She always speaks of her feelings for Macheath, which she uses to excuse her actions, in monetary terms. Apparently she does not love Macheath in the traditional sense, for she talks of the effects of love as being a "bribe" and seems more put out that Polly will now have her husband's money, rather than herself. It does not seem to bother her that she has also lost the man.

There are also a pair of political **allusions** contained in the dialogue, both concerned with the South Sea Bubble. Prime Minister Walpole really got his chance to come to power because of this incident in the early 1720s having to do with the South Sea Company's effort to assume the British national debt. A complicated series of events led to this being a seriously discussed possibility, and as a result stock in the company soared, despite warnings by Walpole and others. A stock market crash ensued and stock in the South Sea Company plummeted from 1,000 pounds per share to 135 pounds. Thousands of investors, many of them of very limited means, were ruined and Parliament and the Cabinet came under scathing criticism. Walpole had not been a member of the Cabinet long enough to acquire the stigma attached to it, and the situation gave him a chance to exercise his financial genius, thus saving England economically. In this scene Lockit mentions that those who act otherwise than "on the foot of interest" are foolish and are in fact their own "bubbles." In itself such a statement might be considered coincidental, but the air which follows, number XLII, is based on the tune of one of the many **ballads** dealings with the South Sea Bubble economic disaster, so it is likely that Gay consciously had the affair in mind when writing the scene.

Scene 2

Having sent Lucy away, Lockit theorizes that Peachum is responsible for the chain of events and temporizes that the key to a successful life is cheating your fellow before he can cheat you. He has a **ballad** ready to demonstrate his contention. Lockit repeats the recurring **theme** that man is a sociable animal of prey who, "According to the custom of the world," has thousands of precedents for cheating his best friends, as he imagines Peachum has done, and as he intends to do unto Peachum in return.

Scene 3

Lockit questions Filch about his master's whereabouts, incidentally commenting on a "great man" who saves the ladies from hanging by helping them become pregnant. Since this scene is unimportant as a device to further the plot, to divulge additional information, or to amuse, and is even barren of a **ballad** (!), we can assume that the **allusion** to a "great man" is again a reference to Walpole and that this is the scene's raison d'etre.

Scene 4

At a gaming-house Macheath, playing cards with Ben Budge and Matt of the Mint, considers the subject of money and the upper class's attitude toward it. This leads his two friends to compare his state with that of the aristocracy. The three make plans to meet later at Marybone.

Macheath is back in business already, planning the evening activities. He also uses the occasion to note that he and his friends are better than their betters because they still have enough honor among themselves to overcome the corruption of the world, an amusing statement coming from a man who is about to rob someone who has beaten him at gaming. He does show himself to be above the habitues of the court, though, when he generously supplies his moneyless friends with funds, professing that he acts upon friendship, instead of talking about acting on friendship and doing nothing.

Scene 5 And 6

In Peachum's lock, Peachum and Lockit discuss the disposal of items stolen during King George II's Coronation (1727). Lockit suggests that if Peachum keeps an eye on Polly, he will discover Macheath's location within the next couple of days, though his friend questions the significance of capturing the highwayman if the prison-keeper's daughter will immediately effect his release. Mrs. Trapes, a woman fond of her liquor, appears for a business conference and innocently reveals the whereabouts of the Captain-he is at Mrs. Coaxer's in Marybone.

In these scenes, a break in the flow of the action ensues, allowing the audience to catch its breath and to start building the suspense again as the refuge of Captain Macheath is about to be revealed.

The action is Scene 5 merely provides another example of the business-like nature of the crooks and underscores Gay's technique of reversal. Peachum and Lockit act as though they are involved in a completely natural profession-they talk about the most amazing crimes (i.e., the Coronation is not seen as a great event, a state celebration, but as an opportunity to steal unmolested) as if completely unaware that what they are doing is not only dishonorable but certainly not the most normal thing in the world. Their ease in the conversation serves to emphasize the disparity with what they are talking about-the manner in which they discuss their subject creates an amusing contrast.

Mrs. Trapes' entrance is used as an excuse to comment on recent actions of Parliament to show that these characters are so involved with gain through the injury of others that they see even benevolent laws as harmful. An Act of 1724 was responsible for cleaning up the Mint, that area in Southwark which had served as a haven for debtors and criminals, and Mrs. Trapes complains that this has caused her business to suffer. She also discloses the fact that she has seen Macheath at Mrs. Coaxer's, thus advancing the plot.

Scene 7

Back at Newgate, Lucy is suffering from jealousy, as she prepares to poison her rival, Polly. Now that Macheath is suddenly in danger again, Gay heightens the suspense even further by placing Polly in danger, too.

Scene 8

The two women greet each other cordially and apologize courteously for their previous antagonistic behavior. After several songs Lucy departs to fetch the poisoned brandy.

As with the previous scenes in which Lucy and Polly confront one another, the humor of Scene 8 derives in large part from the contrast between what is obviously their feelings about each other and the super-civilized manner which they affect. They are too civilized to be sincere, and the underlying attitude is shown by small things such as the contradiction in Polly's pretentious overpoliteness and her more realistic use of language, as when she apologizes for her rude departure when last they met, occasioned by her father's hauling her away. The word "haul'd" is harsh and seems more natural to the two women than the simpering gratuitousness they display. And, of course, the counterpointal singing again is the dramatist's way of poking fun at the operatic form and the highly publicized quarrel between Faustina and Cuzzoni.

Lucy's continual attempts to get Polly to accept a drink builds the scene's suspense (and allows for Lucy's humorously ironic comment that she will be even with the "hypocritic strumpet," when she herself is seen to be acting hypocritically).

Scene 9

While waiting, Polly discloses to the audience that she suspects Lucy's friendly manners. Polly, it seems, has finally learned something about the world around her, for she now realizes that if someone acts in a friendly manner, they must be trying to hide something.

Scene 10

Lucy returns with the liquor. Polly is about to drink when she sees Macheath being brought back to prison and drops her glass. Since Macheath is back in Newgate, Lucy is glad her design has gone awry.

Ironically, Polly is saved by the one thing which could make her most unhappy-the return of Macheath to prison. And because she is so unhappy, Lucy is glad that the poisoning was not successful because it would have been wasted. By their reactions it is made clear who really loves Macheath, thus providing the chance for a happy reunion after the conclusion of the play.

Scene 11

Peachum and Lockit once more escort the prisoner on his way to court, to the distress of the women, who both attempt to get him to recognize her as his sole wife. Macheath responds that neither will have to worry long, for he will soon be dead. Polly and Lucy in turn plead with their fathers to spare the Captain's life, but the two men are adamant and will not give in.

For the first time in the play all five main characters are present on stage at the same time, and as might be expected, their various attitudes are the same as those that they have been expressing throughout the rest of *The Beggar's Opera*. Polly seems to be the only character who has been fairly consistently sincere in her emotions during the entire drama. With the exception of an occasional lapse, her love for Macheath has never really been in doubt, though typically there is a piece of reversal involved in her singing of "Air LIV" in which she laments that before she fell in love every month was May, rather than love making every month seem like May. Love, then, brings unhappiness.

Macheath, too, seems to have a somewhat compassionate nature, as he is undecided as to which "wife" to choose in "Air LIII", since a choice of any kind must unavoidably cause someone to suffer. His easy-going attitude toward life is reflected in his ready acceptance of death: "I go, undismay'd-For death is a debt." It is amusing, and very much in character, that this cool expression of his attitude toward death includes a pun; the words "death" and "debt" were originally pronounced alike.

On the other hand, neither Peachum nor Lockit displays much compassion for their daughters or their "son-in-law." Peachum's attempt to settle the point of which woman will be the legitimate widow sums up their attitude, for he shows no sympathy for Macheath's plight, but instead is interested only in the money involved which might be lost if a lawsuit cannot be prevented.

Scene 12

Lucy and Polly send Filch to follow the trio and report what happens at the trial. This is followed by "A dance of prisoners in chains, etc."

The main point of Scene 12 lies in the absurd contrast between the ridiculous spectacle of the prisoners dancing in their chains and the more "serious" events surrounding the doomed Macheath. By introducing this humorous sight, the playwright seems to be telling his audience that the "serious" events should not be taken seriously, thereby preparing us for the plot manipulation at the end of the play.

Scene 13

Macheath, "in a melancholy posture" in the condemned hold, sings a series of tunes relating the history of his downfall. A Jailor announces the arrival of his friends.

The fragments of ten songs are contained in Macheath's medley, as he recalls how his fondness for women is responsible for his present condition and how he wishes that he had access to money, which could save him from hanging, as it has saved many rich men. Included among the airs Gay draws upon in the Captain's concert are "Chevy Chase," an old Scotch **ballad**, "To old Simon the King," one of Squire Western's favorite tunes in Fielding's *Tom Jones*, and the ever-popular Elizabethan air, "Greensleeves."

Scene 14

Ben Budge and Matt of the Mint hear their leader denounce Jemmy Twitcher for having "peached" him and they agree to honor Macheath's last request-to bring Peachum and Lockit to the gallows.

The loyalty of one's acquaintances is questioned again in Scene 14 when Macheath complains that "even our gang can no more trust one another than other people," a contradiction of the sentiments expressed earlier by several of the gang members. Macheath's declaration has some weight behind it, naturally, since it is based on Jemmy Twitcher's betrayal of his leader; but since we already know that Peachum and Lockit were made aware of his whereabouts by Mrs. Trapes, the exact nature of Twitcher's betrayal is not clear-perhaps this is a lapse on the part of the author. It was Twitcher in Act II, Scene 1 who declared that the criminal class is not "more dishonest than the rest of mankind"-which is exactly Gay's point.

Scene 15

As Ben and Matt depart, Lucy and Polly enter. Once again the Captain refuses to acknowledge his love for either of them and the drama ends as "four wives more" and their children come to see Macheath, who is willingly led off by the sheriff's officers.

Polly continues to vocalize her love; Lucy repeats the concept introduced in Act I that there is nothing more moving than the sight of a man in distress; and Macheath provides a bit of gallows humor by holding up his empty liquor bottle and announcing that his courage "is out."

The arrival of the four additional wives and their children is the crowning point of the scene and makes all of the Captain's pronouncements to Polly and Lucy and all of his observations on marriage even funnier in retrospect.

Scene 16

After Macheath has been taken away, the Player and the Beggar from the introduction return to the stage where the Player wonders if Macheath is really meant to hang. The Beggar replies that he is, in the interest of "strict poetical justice," but the Player complains that such a conclusion would make the piece a tragedy, which is "manifestly wrong, for an opera must end happily." Taking this objection into consideration, the Beggar grants a reprieve, much to the relief of the Player, who states that this will "comply with the taste of the town." The Beggar ironically sums up the meaning of the drama.

The Beggar had intended for the play to end on a note of poetic justice, that is, everyone would get what they deserve, which is why Captain Macheath is led off to be hanged at the conclusion of *The Beggar's Opera*. In this way the Beggar had hoped to impart a "most excellent moral" through his tale. Not only would he thus demonstrate that there is "such a similitude of manners in high and low life, that it is difficult to determine whether ... the fine gentlemen imitate the gentlemen of the road, or the gentlemen of the road the fine gentlemen," he would also have shown that "the lower sort of people have their vices in a degree as well as the rich". Until now most dramas had focused on the upper classes. Furthermore, such a conclusion would have shown that the lower classes "are punish'd" for their vices, a most admirable moral, especially since the upper classes often went unpunished for similar doings, a suitable warning to the lower classes!

In a final ironic reversal, however, the Beggar gives way to the Player's objections that this ending can only be construed a tragedy, a veritable "catastrophe," since operas must end happily, something which clearly goes against the "taste of the town." Gay is mocking that same "taste" when the Beggar agrees that there is no difficulty in adjusting the ending to fit the audience's expectations, because in opera there is no need to follow logic or to pay any attention to the development of either characters or plot-"'tis no matter how absurdly things are brought about." In view of this characteristic of the operatic form it is an easy thing to correct the fault; he simply has a reprieve cried, something for which there were ample precedents in operatic lore and sentimental comedies.

Scene 17

Macheath returns to the problem of two wives and, since he no longer can depend upon the gallows to save him, he chooses Polly, admitting that they were married all along. The play concludes with a dance and a final song.

With the return of the reprieved Captain and the happy reunion with his admitted wife, Polly, the drama can now end on a happy note-literally, as the curtain fittingly comes down on *The Beggar's Opera* with a concluding song.

THE BEGGAR'S OPERA

. . . .

The following essay questions and model answers are intended to suggest various approaches to understanding the meaning and techniques to be found in Gay's *The Beggar's Opera*, to held relate different aspects of the work to one another, to provide a means of review, and to indicate subjects for further research and discussion on the student's part.

Question: What evidence is there that one of Gay's motives for writing *The Beggar's Opera* was to **burlesque** the operatic form currently enjoying such a success on the London stage?

Answer: The best way to answer this question is to examine *The Beggar's Opera* itself, in order to determine whether Gay made any explicit statements within the drama which would indicate that this purpose was to create a **burlesque**, and then to determine whether Gay did indeed employ any common operatic techniques in a **burlesque** manner.

First of all, there is a need to define the terms of the question. According to *Webster's Seventh New Collegiate Dictionary* (Springfield, 1956), an opera is simply "a drama set to music and made up of vocal pieces with orchestral accompaniment and orchestral overtures and interludes." *A Handbook to Literature* (ed. William Flint Thrall and Adison Hibbard, revised by C. Hugh Holman, New York, 1960) is more specific, however: "Opera is musical Drama in the sense that the Dialogue instead of being spoken is sung, to the accompaniment of instrumental music... A play in which incidental music is stressed may be called 'operatic,' but is not true opera if the Dialogue is spoken." Allardyce Nicoll's comment on Sir William Davenant's *Siege of Rhodes* (1656) indicates that the English opera form was a modification of the Italian, for it is "a musical entertainment ... written in rime and designed on the lines of Italian opera to be sung in recitative and aria." Elsewhere, Nicoll notes that, during the eighteenth century, the "**ballad** opera" was known by various names: opera, comic opera, opera-comedy, farcical opera, **ballad** opera, **burlesque** opera, tragi-comi-farcical ballad-opera, tragi-comi-pastoral farcical opera, histori-tragi-comi-ballad opera, comic masque, comedy, dramatic piece, interlude, musical entertainment, and dramatic fable.

A **burlesque** is "mockery usually by caricature," "a witty or derisive usually literary imitation" (*Webster's Seventh*), "characterized by ridiculous exaggeration" (Thrall, Hibbard, and Holman). Furthermore Sylvan Barnet, Morton Berman, and William Burto in *A Dictionary of Literary Terms* (Boston, 1960) state that a **burlesque** "aims to amuse." V.C. Clinton-Baddeley in *The Burlesque Tradition* in the English Theatre after 1660 is also useful for determining these definitions.

As for Gay's purpose in writing *The Beggar's Opera*, it seems obvious from the title of the play alone that the author intended for it to be compared to other "operas." Then, lest his audience miss this hint, he has one of his characters state his position before the drama even begins. In the "Introduction" the Beggar makes clear his humorous attitude toward opera when he says, "I have introduc'd the **similes** that are in all your celebrated opera: the Swallow, the Moth, the Bee, the Ship, the Flower, etc. Besides, I have a prison scene, which the ladies always reckon charmingly pathetick ... I hope I may forgiven, that I have not made my opera throughout unnatural, like those in vogue."

The Beggar's comment that the play was originally meant to celebrate the marriage of James Chanter and Moll Lay, whose names immediately suggest the nature of the tunes which will follow, and his list of "similes," the nature of which indicates that they will be the objects of humor (the very fact that they are cataloged makes an implied comment on the artificiality of the form), are evidence that the following drama will be a parody.

And the actors realized that they were participating in a **burlesque**. On opening night, when the Beggar announced that he would have no recitative, prologue, or epilogue, the spectators felt that they were about to be cheated out of the music which usually preceded an opera and they became somewhat restive, causing the director to ask John Hall, who played the part of Lockit, to go out and apologize to the audience before there was any further disturbance. Hall, flustered by the sudden silence which greeted his appearance, blurted out, "Ladies and gentlemen, we-we-beg you'll not call for first and second music-because you all know, that there is never any music at all in an opera." Such an admission delighted the house and they responded to the rest of the play in good humor.

Turning to the play itself, there is ample evidence that the characters of Polly and Lucy and their squabbles were meant to make fun of the squabble currently being engaged in by England's two leading prima donnas, Faustina and Cuzzoni, a quarrel well-known by the play-goers and referred to in the "Introduction":

"I have observ'd such a nice impartiality to our two ladies, that it is impossible for either of them to take offense." In addition to the improbable events which take place in the drama, of course, there are the sixty-four airs which are included.

And, finally, there is the farcical conclusion to the play. When the Beggar explains that he has had Macheath led off to be hanged in order to demonstrate poetic justice, the Player responds, "The **catastrophe** is manifestly wrong, for an opera must end happily." Recognizing the justice of the Player's objection, the Beggar replies: "in this kind of drama, 'tis no matter how absurdly things are brought about," and immediately proves it by having a reprieve cried and the entire ending ironically reversed.

Clearly, then, Gay did intend to **burlesque** the opera form. He mocks operatic **conventions** and includes enough singing to make his piece at least "operatic" in nature, if not a true opera- which it cannot be, in spite of its title, since the dialogue is not sung. However, since Gay meant to mock the form, it was not necessary for him to follow it exactly, only for him to include enough references to the form for it to be easily recognizable. Then he merely exaggerates those aspects which he feels most vulnerable.

Question2: Discuss the basic technical device Gay uses to create both humor and **satire** in *The Beggar's Opera*.

Answer: The basic technical device which Gay uses to create both humor and **satire** in his work is the simple one of reversal.

First and most obviously, this technique is seen in the inversion of moral values. In general this takes the form of a reversal in the standard attitude toward marriage, as when

Mrs. Peachum exclaims (Act I, Scene 8) that "Our Polly is a sad slut!" not because she has allowed herself to be seduced by Macheath, but because she has married him! For the characters in this drama, seduction is acceptable, marriage to be avoided at all cost as being immoral.

Second, Gay carefully draws a comparison between the upper and lower classes (as Peachum sings in the opening words of the play, "the statesman ... Thinks his trade as honest as mine") to the extent that in the Beggar's words, "you may observe such a similitude of manners in high and low life, that it is difficult to determine whether... the fine gentlemen imitate the gentlemen of the road, or the gentlemen of the road the fine gentlemen."

Third, this equation, together with the moral reversal mentioned above, allows Gay to further his points by creating a new definition of morality, which is, essentially, that it is moral if it is to your own advantage and you do not get caught, and which applies to statesmen and criminals as well. This is brought out in the conversations between Peachum and Lockit, in the casual business-like way crimes are discussed, and in the overt comparisons between the classes used as "precedents" in the dialogue throughout the play.

Fourth, there is the reversal of **conventions** from opera and from sentimental comedy which depends on the audience's familiarity with the dramatic **conventions** being burlesqued and its consequent expectations. A fine example of this is seen at the end of Act I when Polly and Macheath pledge their love to one another, then tear themselves apart. Peachum's dragging the still singing out Polly of Macheath's prison cell, and the "suspenseful" confrontation between Polly and Lucy with the threat of the poisoned drink are similar examples.

Fifth, there is the contrast between the words to the airs being sung and the words to the original tunes. Again, this depends on audience recognition and the contrast between the expected and the delivered. This technique is discussed in greater detail below, in Question 3.

Question: Compare the words of the songs which Gay wrote and the words of the original ballads. What changes has Gay made and what is the effect of these changes?

Answer: From the moment the curtain opens on John Gay's *The Beggar's Opera* to reveal Peachum seated at a desk examining his account ledgers, the importance of music in the play is obvious. Before uttering a word of dialogue, Peachum bursts into song and the dramatist's technique is revealed, for Gay consciously utilizes his tunes to carry much of the meaning of the drama, as well as to provide a source on which a good deal of the humor depends. (Note: interestingly, William Cooke's edition of *Memoirs of Charles Macklin Comedian with the Dramatic Characters, Manners Anecdotes, etc. of the Age in which he Lived*, London, 1804, p. 60, improbably claims: "To this opera there was no music originally intended to accompany the songs, till Rich, the Manager, suggested it on the second last Rehearsal. The junto of wits, who regularly attended, one and all, objected to it; and it was given up till the Duchess of Queensberry accidentally hearing of it, attended herself the next rehearsal, when it was tried and universally approved of." Because of the playwright's obvious plan for the songs, this story is probably not true.)

In the "Introduction" in front of the curtain before the piece itself actually begins, the Beggar explains his purpose in writing the play by referring to **ballad** singers and to Italian operas, thereby preparing his audience for a **parody** of the operatic

91

form and the use of **ballads** as a parodying device. It is fitting, therefore, that the first words of *The Beggar's Opera* are sung. "Air I" is not just an incidental song used to make fun of singing on the stage, though, for it contains a statement of the drama's basic **theme**, sets the pattern the play is to follow, and establishes the light, satiric tone of the work.

When Peachum sings that "Each neighbor abuses his brother" and "All professions be-rogue one another," he is humorously stating the playwright's **theme**, since it is clear throughout the play that Gay is saying that men are dishonest rogues on all levels of society-the only difference being in the manner in which they display their dishonesty and the punishment they receive if they are caught. Proclaiming a similarity between thieves, priests, and lawyers, the song concludes with the amusing observation that the statesmen thinks his trade as honest as Peachum's, a dealer in stolen goods and a "peacher" who sells information on the members of his own gang in order to collect rewards. Even while performing the most outlandish acts and treacheries upon one another, the characters in the drama continually stress that they are behaving no differently from the most respected members of society and much of the fun in the play comes from hearing the criminals and whores excuse their actions in song in this way as they reverse society's normal moral codes with their observations that dishonesty is not merely commonly accepted, it is the best policy.

In addition to serving as a medium for expressing Gay's satirical attack on the upper class, the **ballad** also provides an example of the humor found in the drama which is based on the contrast between Gay's words and the original version of the song. In this instance the air is set to the melody of a popular **ballad**, "Unconstant Roger," which begins:

And old Woman Cloathed in Grey, Whose Daughter was charming and young, But Chanc'd to be once led astray, By Roger's false flattering Tongue. With whom she too often had been, Abroad in the meadows and Field.

"Unconstant Roger" was firmly established in the public domain when *The Beggar's Opera* was first presented, having appeared in the seventeen or eighteen editions of Playford's collection of ballads, *The Dancing Master*, between 1650 and 1728, and it was familiar to all of the audience. Playing on the spectators' expectations, Gay's version contrasts amusingly with its original. So it is with most of the airs in the play-the words of Gay's version would be quite familiar. The contrast with the expected produces much of the humor in the drama. (Note: the original versions of many of the songs Gay borrows are recorded in Thomas D'Urfey's collection. *Wit and Mirth*, or *Pills to Purge Melancholy*, London, 1698, commonly referred to as *Pills* or *Pills to Purge Melancholy*, or in Playford's *The Dancing Master*, various edition, 1650–1728. Frank Kidson's *The Beggar's Opera: Its Predecessors and Successors*, Cambridge, 1922, lists the sources for most of the airs found in *The Beggar's Opera*.)

Finally, "Air I" sets a pattern which the dramatist follows through the rest of the play: songs are used either to make a comment which is followed by dialogue giving evidence that the contention related in the **ballad** is true, or the song itself is used to present evidence that a previous observation is valid. Peachum declares in "Through all the employments of life" that all professions are similarly corrupt, then draws a comparison between the way he earns his living and the lawyer's profession as proof that what he has sung is true.

All in all, then, there is a marvelous diversity of effects which Gay accomplishes with "Air I". Not only does the **ballad** suit the author's purpose in parodying opera, it carries his **theme**, contains humor, and establishes the basis for the structural pattern he will employ in his work-and all in the opening moments of the play. That this is merely where Gay starts in *The Beggar's Opera* is a mark of his dramatic ingenuity. And the same things can be said about almost every air sung throughout the entire drama. The changes Gay has made in the wording of his airs in comparison to their originals was the source of his success and popularity for eighteenth-century play-goers.

Question: What political **allusions** are found in *The Beggar's Opera*?

Answer: There are political **allusions** through the entire action of *The Beggar's Opera* from Peachum's singing of "Air I" on ("the statesmen, because he's so great"). Most of the **allusions** refer to Prime Minister Sir Robert Walpole.

Although many of the political references are generally simply equating the actions and morality of statesmen and criminals as part of Gay's overall message ("'Tis our mutual interest; 'tis for the interest of the world"), there are numerous **allusions** to Walpole specifically. For instance, there is continual commentary about "great" men in politics whose actions parallel those of the gang members: "like great statesmen, we encourage those who betray their friends," Peachum reminds Lockit in Act II, Scene 10. Walpole was commonly referred to as "the great man," so the eighteenth-century audience would have readily understood all such **allusions** as applying to the Prime Minister.

Likewise, the audience would have recognized the aliases of Bob Booty as being **allusions** to Walpole, Robin of Bagshot, Gorgon, Bluff Bob, and Carbuncle would all have been seen as references to Walpole. Furthermore, Bagshot Heath (the haunt of Robin of Bagshot) was a favorite locale outside London for robbers to lurk, and the audience would be quick to equate Bagshot Heath with the Houses of Parliament.

Some critics have seen a political analogy in the relationship between Macheath, Peachum, and the members of the gang as expressed in Act II, Scene 2. Macheath is the acknowledged ruler of the organization, like King George II, but it is Peachum, like Walpole, who controls the treasury and, therefore, is the real power.

The dialogue in Act III, Scene 1 between Lucy and her father, Lockit, also contains a pair of political allusions, both concerned with the South Sea Bubble. Prime Minister Walpole really got his chance to come to power because of this incident in the early 1720s, having to do with the South Sea Company's effort to assume the British national debt. A complicated series of events led to this being a seriously discussed possibility, and as a result stock in the company soared, despite warnings by Walpole and others. A stock market crash ensued and stock in the South Sea Company plummeted from 1,000 pounds per share to 135 pounds. Thousands of investors, many of them of very limited means, were ruined and Parliament and the Cabinet came under scathing criticism. Walpole had not been a member of the Cabinet long enough to acquire the stigma attached to it, and the situation gave him a chance to exercise his financial genius, thus saving England economically. In this scene Lockit mentions that those who act otherwise than "on the foot of interest" are foolish and are in fact their own "bubbles." In itself such a statement might be considered coincidental, but the air which follows, number XLII, is based on the tune of one of the many **ballads** dealing with the South Sea Bubble economic disaster, so it is likely that Gay consciously had the affair in mind when writing the scene.

Finally, the Lockit/Peachum quarrel in Act II is related to the quarrel between Walpole and Lord Townsend, according to the historical evidence cited by Jean B. Kern in "A Note on The Beggar's Opera" (Philological Quarterly, XVII, 1938, pp. 411–413).

In addition there are incidental political **allusions** scattered through the drama. Peachum and Lockit complain that the government is in arrears in payment of rewards for betraying fellow gang members; Mrs. Trapes is upset because the government passed the Act of 1724, cleaning up the Mint, that area is Southwark which had been a haven for criminals and debtors; in Act 11, Scene 10 it is stated that all courtiers react defensively when they hear the word bribe-and the implication is that they have good reason to act in such a manner; and the King's Coronation is discussed as having been a perfect place for illegal activities by Peachum and Lockit in Act III, Scene 7.

The purpose behind Gay's many political **allusions** in *The Beggar's Opera* is threefold: (1) to attack Prime Minister Robert Walpole personally; (2) to attack the general corruption and abuses of the current government; and (3) to emphasize Gay's contention that there is really very little to differentiate between the activities and morality of the criminal classes and the upper classes. The most immediate results of these **allusions** was the banning of Gay's follow-up to *The Beggar's Opera*, Polly, the next year, and ultimately in the passage of the Licensing Act of 1737 which placed the English stage under the control of the Lord Chamberlain.

Question: How does Gay develop the characters in *The Beggar's Opera*?

Answer: For all practical purposes, the answer to this question is that Gay does not develop the characters in *The Beggar's Opera*.

The reasons for the lack of character development in the drama are essentially quite simple. First, because of the nature of comedy, the author seldom wants the audience to identify with his characters as he would when writing a tragedy, for he wants the audience to be able to view the action more objectively, to be able to divorce themselves from the characters, thus allowing them to laugh at whatever befalls his creations.

Another factor to be taken into consideration in explaining the lack of characterization in *The Beggar's Opera* is Gay's purpose in writing this particular drama. The dramatist was interested in burlesquing the then popular operatic form, and he wanted to create a political and social **satire**. Neither of these motives requires characterization to any extent. Indeed, as with comedy, it is probably better not to have much characterization at all, for the playwright does not want us to be involved with the characters as people. Since he wants us to be interested in matters completely divorced from characterization, it is better for him to deal with flat, superficial characters, stereotypes at best. Peachum and Lockit, for example, are stereotypes of the middle class businessman who thinks of everything in terms of personal profit. They have no understanding of their daughters' feelings, and no sympathy for anyone.

Mrs. Peachum is really a stereotype in reverse. She is a model of the sentimental comedy mother, but her moral standards are just the reverse. Like most of the other characters in the play, she is basically selfish in nature and unsympathetic.

Lucy is a female counterpart of her father, Lockit. The only real difference is that she is momentarily swayed by the force of her emotions.

Polly is the typical mindless sentimental heroine who is ready to defy everyone in order to marry the man she loves, though her idealized version of love makes her only truly admirable quality appear ridiculous, even in contrast with the unfeeling mob about her.

The members of Macheath's gang and the women of the town are not developed as characters either. With the exception of Filch, who shows a bit of initiative, and Ben Budge and Matt of the Mint, both of whom demonstrate a degree of loyalty to their Captain, all of these characters serve only to demonstrate the superficiality, avarice, and disloyalty of mankind.

Of all the characters in *The Beggar's Opera*, only Captain Macheath is developed to any degree at all, and he essentially remains a dissolute Restoration rake, albeit a lower class rake. The only things which remove Macheath from the stereotype category are his admitted love for Polly (in spite of his temporary indiscretions) and his interest in and loyalty to the members of his gang, whom he gives both money and good advice, intended for their benefit.

Again, the very fact that these characters are never developed suits Gay's purpose, for he does not want us to become interested in their difficulties except as a means of expressing his own feelings and as a source of humor. Perhaps the reason that Captain Macheath is the only character in *The Beggar's Opera* who shows any depth (to be distinguished from development, since he does not really develop in the drama) is to create a bit of interest on the audience's part so that they care what happens to him at the end of the play, allowing Gay to produce an absurd conclusion which at the same time will please his audience.

Question: Compare Bertolt Brecht's The Threepenny Opera with Gay's *The Beggar's Opera*.

Answer: There can be no doubt that Bertolt Brecht, the modern German dramatist (1898–1956), patterned his *The Threepenny Opera* (Die Dreigroschenoper, 1928) after Gay's *The Beggar's Opera*. As Lotte Lenya, wife of composer Kurt Weill and the singer/actress who played the part of Ginny Jenny in the original production, relates in "That was a Time!" (Theatre Arts, May, 1956), there was currently a revival of Gay's play in London, a fact brought to Brecht's attention by Elisabeth Hauptmann, Brecht's secretary. Hauptmann sent for a copy of the drama and translated it for Brecht, who then decided to write a modern version of the play. Deciding that the music was in needs of modernizing, too, he called in Kurt Weill as collaborator.

Brecht is considered an innovator, himself, and he did make changes in Gay's work. The story remains basically the same, but Brecht believed in using the stage as a place for the expression of his Communistic ideas, so he uses his original as the starting place for a **satire** on what he calls "bourgeois conceptions," both in terms of the contents of those conceptions and the way in which the contents are presented. This, as Brecht explains in his production notes for the play, leads him to change the characters somewhat. Peachum, for example, is no longer just a stereotype of the modern middle-class businessman, he becomes a character filled with angst, he has no hopes and merely collects money as a way of following current trends. Brecht also emphasizes the parallel between the bourgeois (not the "upper class") and the criminal class by having his actors and actresses dress and act (and perhaps be a little portly and staid) like ordinary shopkeepers.

Besides the new songs and characterizations (Polly becomes a virtuous and agreeable young lady), there are additional minor changes. Lockit is replaced by Brown, the London Chief of Police, the gang becomes more obviously "pretend" beggars using their profession as a front for Chicago gangster-like activities in modern London, and Brecht introduces the use of boards on which are projected the titles of the scenes. Brecht explains the use of these boards as part of his literalization of the theatre which, like his explanation for including two prison scenes (having to do with his concept of an "**epic**" theatre) and the use of a mounted messenger, grows out of his theories about the theatre. (Additional information on Brecht and his theories can be obtained by consulting John Willett's translations of some of Brecht's many volumes of critical writing, *Brecht on Theatre*, New York, 1964, and *The Mesingkauf Dialogues*, London, 1965, as well as the numerous sources in German. Willet's *The Theatre of Bertolt Brecht*, New York, 1959, Martin Esslin's *Brecht: The Man and His Work*, New York, revised 1971, Erika Munk's anthology of eighteen critical pieces on Brecht which appeared in *The Drama Review*, Brecht, New York, 1972, and Charles R. Lyons's *Bertolt Brecht: The Despair and the Polemic*, Carbondale, 1968 all discuss Brecht's art in general and *The Threepenny Opera* specifically.)

Although a popular success (it too, was made into a movie), to large part due to the songs of Kurt Weill, *The Threepenny Opera* is not considered as funny as its original by many critics, though there is, naturally enough, disagreement about this, and Brecht's purposes were somewhat different.

Besides *The Threepenny Opera*, the influence of *The Beggar's Opera* can be seen in other modern writings. Duke Ellington wrote the score for a Broadway musical, *The Beggar's Holiday*, and many critics trace the origins of our modern "musicals" back to Gay's play. And there is a whole sub-genre of literature which is related to *The Beggar's Opera*, that of the underworld. One of the most recent examples of this is Anthony Burgess' novel, *A Clockwork Orange* (1962), with its liberal use of slang (some created by Burgess) and low-life characters and disreputable activities normally associated with the criminal classes. Whether or not such novels owe their existence specifically to Gay's *The Beggar's Opera* or whether they grew out of the same kind of background (see the section on Wild's activities and literary reactions to him in "Introduction to *The Beggar's Opera*: Background" above) is a question which might be fruitfully pursued. The answer is probably that they grew out of a common background, but that *The Beggar's Opera* is now a part of that background and, therefore, does still exert its influence on literature.

THE BEGGAR'S OPERA

. . . .

The answers to the questions listed above are meant to be used by the student as a guide to how to approach his study of *The Beggar's Opera*: they are not meant to take the place of the student's own thinking and research. Below are some additional questions that will involve further independent research on the part of the student, and which will lead the student to a better understanding of the drama.

1. Examine the place of *The Beggar's Opera* in the historical perspective of English drama. The numerous literary histories listed in the Selected Bibliography would have been a good starting place for this question, though an examination of plays referred to in those volumes would give added depth to the study.

2. Compare *The Beggar's Opera* with a typical Italian opera of the same period. Which **conventions** has Gay singled out to **parody**? Is his parody successful? Does the opera form provide a legitimate source to be attacked? In other words, are the things Gay makes fun of suitable to be

satirized because they are unrealistic or excessive-or are these elements valid within the operatic tradition?

In answering this question there are numerous Italian operas which the student might consider. English operas would serve as well, and might include such early pieces as William D'Avenant's The *Siege of Rhodes*, 1656, or works by Dryden, or later operas such as Thomas Clayton's version of *Arisone*, 1705, Buononcini's *Camilla*, 1706, or *Pyrrhus and Demetrius*, 1708, or *Rinaldo and Arminda*, 1711. Other **burlesques** of the form such as Richard Estcourt's *Prunella*, 1708, and Joseph Addison's *Rosamond*, 1701, might also provide interesting perspectives. And critical attacks by John Dennis, Addison [see especially the *Spectator*, #18, 21 March 1711, for example], and other critics would be useful in this study. An ambitious student might even carry the study up to the modern theatre, for the operatic form is still under attack for many of the same reasons as it was in Gay's day. The form also has its defenders, of course, and moderns such as Gian Carlo Monetti have defended the opera vigorously. The outcome of an extended examination along these lines might even lead the student into an understanding of the nature of art and the use of conventions, an essentially unrealistic set of devices commonly accepted.

3. How does Gay use quotations, paraphrasings, and literary **allusions** in *The Beggar's Opera*? An obvious place to start here is with Shakespeare.

4. Is *The Beggar's Opera* really an opera? The answer to this question would involve a discussion of the elements of opera-what are the characteristics of opera

[is an opera merely a play with singing?] and are these characteristics present in *The Beggar's Opera*, or might it better be termed something else!

5. In 1775 Richard Brinsley Sheridan wrote a "comic opera," *The Duenna*. Compare and contrast this work with *The Beggar's Opera*: how are they alike and how are they different? What does this tell you about the authors' purposes?

6. Trace the historical influences of *The Beggar's Opera*. Can Gay's influence still be found in contemporary writings?

7. Do you as a modern student of *The Beggar's Opera* find the play amusing? Why, or why not? What does this tell you about the differences between the eighteenth century and the twentieth century? About the play itself? About Gay's ability as dramatist? About the nature of comedy? About yourself?

THE BEGGAR'S OPERA

....

SURVEY OF SOURCE MATERIAL ON GAY'S "THE BEGGAR'S OPERA"

The standard edition of Gay's work is *The Poetical Works of John Gay* (including *The Beggar's Opera*), edited by G. C. Faber (Oxford University Press, London, 1926). There are numerous other additions available, most of which are adequate, in part because of the unusual publishing history of *The Beggar's Opera*. The play first appeared in print in 1728 (the first octavo edition, J. Watts, authorized publisher), but unlike many other literary works of the period, the editions of *The Beggar's Opera* are essentially the same, there being very little "pirating" of Gay's play unauthorized publishers. Also, as a result perhaps, the earliest editions are generally error-free and differ very little from edition to edition. Most modern editions follow the Q Quarto, the "third edition," based on the last edition newly-set during Gay's life.

John Gay: Favorite of the Wits (Durham, N. C., 1940), by William Henry Irving, is the standard biography of Gay.

In reviewing criticism of Gay and *The Beggar's Opera* it is unfortunate that with a few notable exceptions, there are few outstanding studies of Gay's techniques, or of the play itself. Among those examinations which the student may find most useful there are four categories: (1) the history of the play, (2) the form of the play, (3) the drama's place in the pastoral tradition, and (4) Gay's purpose in writing *The Beggar's Opera*.

(1) Those studies which trace the history of the play, i.e., its background, sources, influences, and so forth, include Charles E. Pearce's *Polly Peachum and The Beggar's Opera* (London, 1913), an amusing pot pourri of history, anecdotes, and criticism which says as much as most of the other studies of this drama, yet manages not to take itself too seriously; and Frank Kidson's *The Beggar's Opera: Its Predecessors and Successors*, (London, 1922) which is not very scholarly either, in giving a general overview of the literary ancestors and conditions in England leading to *The Beggar's Opera* with a short section dealing with the drama's successors and including a listing of the origins for the play's airs. Two shorter pieces also throw some light on the drama's creation: in "A Note on The Beggar's Opera," in *Philological Quarterly*, XVII (1938), pp. 411–413, Jean B. Kerr cites historical evidence relating the Lockit/Peachum quarrel in Act II to Walpole's quarrel with Lord Townsend, and James Sutherland's "The Beggar's Opera," in the *Times Literary Supplement* for April 25, 1935 (p. 272), finds that the anecdote that Swift suggested the Newgate opera is unlikely and suggests that Gay's interest in the career of Jonathan Wild is a more likely source.

(2) The "operatic" form of *The Beggar's Opera* is examined in fairly exhaustive detail by Arthur V. Berger in

"*The Beggar's Opera*, the Burlesque, and Italian Opera" (*Music and Letters*, XVII, 1936, pp. 93–105) as part of his explanation of one of Gay's purposes in writing the play as being a burlesque of the operatic form; Bertrand Harris Bronson's "*The Beggar's Opera*: Studies in the Comic" (University of *California Publications in English*, VIII, No. 2, 1941, pp. 197–231, and reprinted in Facets of the Enlightenment, Berkeley and Los Angeles, 1968) which examines Gay's use of **irony** and suggests that the drama's immediate popularity resulted from the audience's recognition of the tunes used; and the exhaustive study, **Ballad** Opera (New York, 1937) by Edmond McAdoo Gagey, which places *The Beggar's Opera* in the **ballad** opera tradition, as well as examining the form and its development.

(3) The place of *The Beggar's Opera* in the pastoral tradition is the subject of a section of William Empson's *Some Versions of the Pastoral* (New York, 1938) and Samuel H. Joseloffs Princeton University doctoral dissertation, *John Gay and the Eighteenth-Century Pastoral Tradition*.

(4) And finally, Gay's motivation for writing *The Beggar's Opera* is the subject of speculation in Sven M. Armen's *John Gay, Social Critic* (New York, 1954), and in James Sutherland's "John Gay" (in Essays Presented to George Sherburn, Oxford, 1949, pp. 201–214), both of which propose Gay's social attitudes as a motivating force; and in C.F. Burgoess's "Political Satire: John Gay's *The Beggar's Opera* (*The Midwest Quarterly*, 6, 1965, pp. 265–276).

For the best feeling for the background to *The Beggar's Opera* the student might examine general studies such as W. J. Bate's

From Classic to Romantic: Premises of Taste in Eighteenth-Century England (Cambridge, Mass., 1948), standard background of the period, Augustan Age (London and New York, 1950), A. H. Humphries' *The Augustan World: Life and Letters in Eighteenth-Century England* (London, 1954), Joseph Wood Krutch's study of comedy in relation to the age, *Comedy and Conscience after the Restoration* (New York, 1949), and James E. Tobin's *Eighteenth Century Literature and Its Cultural Background* (New York, 1939).

There are numerous historical (political) studies of the eighteenth century which are quite good, but for literary histories of Britain during Gay's time, the standard works are Bonamy Dobree's *English Literature in the Early Eighteenth Century: 1700–1740* (Oxford, 1959, Vol. VII of the Oxford History of English Literature) and George Sherburn's section in *A Literary History of England* (ed. Albert C. Baugh, New York, 1948, London, 1950), "The Restoration and Eighteenth Century, 1660–1789." R. C. Churchill has also published a general literary history, English Literature of the Eighteenth Century (London, 1953).

For bibliographies covering the eighteenth century, the standard work is Ronald S. Crane's *English Literature 1660–1800: A Bibliography of Modern Studies Compiled for Philological Quarterly* (Princeton, 1950. Vol. I contains studies from 1926 to 1938, Vo. II, 1939–1950, Vol. III, 1951–1956, and Vol. IV, 1957–1960). The July issues of *Philological Quarterly* are a continuation of this bibliography.

Because *The Beggar's Opera* is a comedy, the student might gain additional understanding of the play from examining it in light of various theories regarding why people laugh, what is the nature of comedy, and so on. Among the psychological interpreters of the comic are Sigmund Freud, really the first to investigate wit and laughter from a psychological point of view ("Wit and Its Relation to the Unconscious," trans. A. A. Brill, *Basic Writings of Sigmund Freud*, New York, 1938), Henry Bergson in his influential study, *Laughter* (New York, 1913), and more recent writings of Morris W. Brody ("The Meaning of Laughter," *Psychoanalytic Quarterly*, 1950) and Sandor Ferenczi ("The PsAchoanalysis of Wit and the Comical," Further Contributions to Psychoanalysis, London, 1950). Literary insights into the nature of comedy are explored in volumes by Bertrand H. Bronson in *Studies in the Comic* (Berkeley and Los Angeles, 1941) which includes *The Beggar's Opera* among the works of literature examined, Albert S. *Cook in The Dark Voyage and the Golden Mean* (Cambridge, Mass., 1949), Richard Eberhart in "Tragedy as Limitation: Comedy as Control and Resolution" (in Tulane Drama Review, 1962), Northrop Frye in "The Argument of Comedy" (English Institute Essays, New York, 1949-see also his *Anatomy of Criticism*) which is an interesting view of comedy in terms of stereotypes of archetypes having an anthropological basis, and William Hazlitt in *The English Comic Writers* (New York, 1910). Two studies specifically dealing with eighteenth-century comedy are also interesting: John W. Draper's "The Theory of the Comic in Eighteenth-Century England" (*Journal of English and German Philology*, XXXVII, 1938, pp. 207–223) which concludes from a review of contemporary statements about comedy that the eighteenth-century theory of comedy followed the tenets of the neo-classical desire to ridicule, but that in practice the tendency was a movement toward sentimentalism; and M. Stuart Tave's *The Amiable Humorist* (Chicago, 1960), a study of comic theory and criticism in the eighteenth and nineteenth centuries. For an anthology which contains a representative sampling of comic theories from Aristotle to the present, Robert W. Corrigan's Comedy: *Meaning and Form* (San Francisco, 1965) is useful.

Another interesting perspective which can help the student gain insights into *The Beggar's Opera* can be found by examining the history of the English theatre which preceded Gay's work. A general understanding of the British stage is presented in The London Stage: *A Critical Introduction* (Carbondale, edited by Emmett L. Avery and including essays by the editor, A. H. Scouton, George Winchester Stone, Jr., and C. B. Hogan, all specialists in the historic conditions under which eighteenth-century dramas were performed; Sir Ifor Evans' *A Short History of English Drama* (Boston, 1965) which is limited, but provides a quick overview; *From Dryden to Johnson* (London, 1957), edited by Boris Ford in the *Pelican Guide to English Literature* series, which is similar to the Evans volume, though it goes into somewhat more detail regarding individual authors; and Allardyce Nicoll's *A History of English Drama*, 1660–1900 (Cambridge, Mass., 1952–59, Vols. I-III), which is a standard literary history commenting on individual dramatists, plays, staging, and acting, and includes helpful bibliographies, *The Development of the Theatre* (New York, 1958, revised), and *The English Theatre* (New York, 1936), both of which provide a historical and critical overview. Also of interest are several studies which detail the English theatre before Gay, giving us a better appreciation of his originality and the literary subjects of his **satire**. These include Bonamy Dobree's older study of the comedy of the Restoration period, *Restoration Comedy* (Oxford, 1924); Thomas H. Fujimura's The Restoration Comedy of Wit (Princeton, 1952) which argues that Restoration comedy used wit to attack moral issues; Kathleen Lynch's study of the influences, primarily French, which helped shape comedy in Britain previous to Gay, *The Social Mode of Restoration Comedy* (Ann Arbor, 1926); and John Harold Wilson's *Preface to Restoration Drama* (Boston, 1965) which beautifully portrays the conditions during the reign of Charles II under which dramas were performed.

Perhaps even more valuable to the student of *The Beggar's Opera* is a clear picture of the drama being written by Gay's contemporaries, for this demonstrates just how innovative he was. There are numerous literary histories dealing specifically with the eighteenth century which provide information of this sort. Frederick S. Boas' *An Introduction to Eighteenth-Century Drama, 1700–1790* (London, 1953) is a standard examination of English drama during Gay's time, as is Allardyce Nicoll's *A History of Early Eighteenth-Century Drama, 1700–1750* (Cambridge University Press, 1929). Also useful are two volumes by George H. Nettleton, *English Drama of the Restoration* and *Eighteenth Century* (New York, 1914), which is a valuable standard examination of the types of plays presented during the eighteenth century, though the study is now somewhat dated; and a standard college textbook co-authored by Arthur E. Case and revised by George Winchester Stone, Jr., *British Dramatists from Dryden to Sheridan* (New York, 1969), which includes examinations of the various types of drama presented in the eighteenth century, together with representative plays. More specialized volumes dealing with the British theatre at Gay's time are F. W. Bateson's *English Comic Drama, 1700–1750* (Oxford, 1925), a standard study of British comic drama contemporary with Gay; Joseph Wood Krutch's *Comedy and Conscience after the Restoration* (New York, 1926, reprinted 1949 and 1967), which is a historical study of the relationship between eighteenth-century comedy and eighteenth-century life, including behavior and conditions in the playhouses, *John Loftis's Comedy and Society from Congreve to Fielding* (Stanford, 1959), which is an important examination of the relationship between the presentation of stereotypes and plots and shifts in the English social classifications in the early eighteenth century, and Loftis's *The Politics of Drama in Augustan England* (Oxford, 1963), which is a study of how British political thought and action were reflected on stage. A well-documented study of trends in critical taste, Charles Harold Gray's *Theatrical Criticism in London to 1795* (New York, 1931) gives additional insight into the milieu in which Gay worked. Finally, there are two collections of miscellaneous material which help the student understand the British stage in the 1700s: John Genest's *Some Account of the English Stage from the Restoration in 1660 to 1830* (10 vols., Bath, 1932), a chronological history of stage performances interspersed with critical commentary, though limited because it includes only about half of the performances given during this period; and The London Stage, 1660–1800, *A Calendar of Plays, Entertainments, and After-pieces, together with Casts, Box-receipts, and Contemporary Comment* (Carbondale, 1960–69), an invaluable eleven volume collection of material for those interested in English stage history compiled by W. B. Van Lennep, E. L. Avery, A. H. Scouton, George Winchester Stone, Jr., and C. B. Hogan.

ANNOTATED BIBLIOGRAPHY

· ·

JOHN GAY

Gay, John. *The Beggar's Opera. Contained in The Poetical Works of John Gay*, ed. G.C. Faber. Oxford University Press: London, 1926. The standard edition of Gay's works.

Armens, Sven M. John Gay, *Social Critic*. King's Crown Press: New York, 1954. An examination of the motivation behind Gay's writing and his success.

Berger, Arthur V. "*The Beggar's Opera*, the **Burlesque**, and Italian Opera," Music and Letters, XVII (1936), pp. 93–105. An informative examination of one of Gay's purposes in writing *The Beggar's Opera*.

Bronson, Bertrand Harris. "*The Beggar's Opera*: Studies in the Comic," *University of California Publications in English*, VIII, No. 2 (1941), pp. 197–231. An important examination of Gay's use of **irony** in *The Beggar's Opera* which suggests that the drama's immediate popularity resulted from the audience's recognition of the tunes used. Sources for the tunes are given. Reprinted in Facets on the Englightenment (University of California Press, Berkeley and Los Angeles, 1968).

Burgess, C. F. "Political **Satire**: John Gay's *The Beggar's Opera*." *The Midwest Quarterly* 6 (1965), pp. 265–276.

_____ "John Gay and Polly and a letter to the King," *Philological Quarterly*, 47: 596–8 (October 1965).

Empson, William. Some Versions of the Pastoral. W. W. Norton: New York, 1938. Includes *The Beggar's Opera* in an examination of the pastoral tradition.

Gagey, Edmond McAdoo. **Ballad** *Opera. Columbia University Press*: New York 1937. An examination of the **ballad** opera form and the place of *The Beggar's Opera* in the tradition and development of the form.

Griffith, Benjamin W. ed. *The Beggar's Opera. Barron's Educational Series*: Great Neck: 1962. This edition of Gay's play includes stage directions and an interesting introductory section which discusses the history of the play, staging, costuming, etc.

Herbert, A. P. Mr. *Gay's London: Ernest Benn*. London, 1949.

Irving, William Henry. *John Gay: Favorite of the Wits*. Duke University Press: Durham, N. C., 1940. The standard critical biography of Gay.

_____ *John Gay's London*. Harvard University Press: Cambridge, Mass., 1928.

Joseloff, *Samuel H. John Gay and the Eighteenth-Century Pastoral Tradition*. (Dissertation, Princeton University).

Kern, Jean B. "A Note on *The Beggar's Opera*," *Philological Quarterly*, XVII (1938), pp. 411–413. Cites historical evidence relating the Lockit/ Peachum quarrel in Act II to Walpole's quarrel with Lord Townsend.

Kidson, Frank. "*The Beggar's Opera*: Its Predecessors and Successors." Cambridge University Press: London, 1922. A general overview of the literary ancestors and conditions in England leading to *The Beggar's Opera* with a short section dealing with the drama's successors and including a listing of origins for the play's airs.

Pearce, *Charles E. Polly Peachum and the Beggar's Opera*. London, 1913. Amusing, filled with history and anecdotes about Gay and his work.

Roberts, Edgar V., ed. *The Beggar's Opera. Music ed. Edward Smith. Regents Restoration Drama Series*. University of Nebraska Press: Lincoln, Neb.

Schultz, William E. *Gay's Beggar's Opera. Yale University Press*: New Haven, 1923.

Sherman, Dorothy L. "Ambivalence in the Theatre Plays of John Gay." (Dissertion, Stanford University, 1969).

Sherwin, Oscar. *Mr. Gay*. John Day: New York, 1929.

Sutherland, James R. "John Gay," *Eighteenth-Century English Literature: Modern Essays in Criticism, ed. James L. Clifford. Oxford University Press*: New York, 1959.

____ "John Gay," *Essays Presented to George Sherburn*. Oxford, 1949, pp. 201–214. Discusses Gay's social attitudes.

____ "*The Beggar's Opera*," *Times Literary Supplement* (April 25, 1935), p. 272. Finds that the anecdote that Swift suggested the Newgate opera is unlikely and suggests that Gay's interest in the career of Jonathan Wild is a more likely source.

Wardle, R. M. "Hazlitt on *The Beggar's Opera*," *South Atlantic Quarterly*. 70:256–64 (Spring 1971).

Weisstein, Ulrich, "Brecht's Victorian Version of Gay: Imitation and Originality in the Dreigroschenoper." *Comparative Literature Studies* 7 ((1970): 314–35. Determines that the relationship between Gay's *The Beggar's Opera* and Brecht's *The Threepenny Opera* are even closer than generally realized, though there are differences: "From a moral point of view, the *Beggar's Opera* is a topical political **satire** which seeks to demonstrate that in Gay's England high and low society were equally corrupt ... [*The Threepenny Opera*] is a universal **satire** which makes little reference to the contemporary German situation. It was Brecht's main concern to show that actually the bourgeois is a robber, just as the robber is a bourgeois." Weisstein also discusses differences in the music used by the two authors.

The Eighteenth Century

Bate, W. J. *From Classic to Romantic: Premises of Taste in Eighteenth-Century England*. Cambridge, Mass., 1948.

Brack, O. M., Jr., et al. "English Literature, 1660–1800: A Current Bibliography," *Philological Quarterly*, 48:289–415. A good source for material on the century and Gay.

Butt, John. *The Augustan Age*. London and New York, 1950. A standard background of the period.

Camden, Carroll, ed. *Restoration and Eighteenth-Century Literature: Essays Collected in Honor of Arthur Ellicott Case*, Ann Arbor, 1952.

Churchill, R. C. *English Literature of the Eighteenth Century*. London 1953. A general literary history.

Clifford, J. L., ed. *Eighteenth Century English Literature: Modern Essays in Criticism*. New York: Oxford University Press, 1959.

Crane, Ronald S. and others, eds. *English Literature 1660–1800: A Bibliography of Modern Studies Compiled for Philological Quarterly*. Princeton, 1950. The standard bibliography for studies, 1926–1960: Vol. I: 1926–1938; Vol. II: 1939–1950; Vol. III: 1951–1956; Vol. IV: 1957–1960. See July issues of Philological Quarterly for continuation.

Dobree, Bonamy. *English Literature in the Early Eighteenth Century: 1700–1740*. Oxford, 1959.

The standard literary history, Vo. VII of the Oxford History of English Literature.

Humphries, A. H. *The Augustan World: Life and Letters in Eighteenth-Century England*. London, 1954. Gives a feeling for the literary life in eighteenth-century England.

Krutch, Joseph Wood. *Comedy and Conscience after the Restoration*. New York, 1949. One of the best studies of comedy in relation to the age.

Plumb, J. H. *England in the Eighteenth Century*. Baltimore, 1950. A general history of eighteenth-century England.

Sherburn, George. "The Restoration and Eighteenth Century, 1660–1789," in A Literary History of England, ed. Albert C. Baugh. New York, 1948, London, 1950. A standard examination of the literature of the period.

Stephen, Sir Leslie. *A history of English Thought in the Eighteenth Century*. 2 vols. London, 1902.

Tobin James E. *Eighteenth Century English Literature and its Cultural Background*. New York, 1939.

Comedy

Bergson, Henry, *Laughter*. New York: Macmillan, 1913. An examination of the nature of laughter.

Brody, Morris W. "The Meaning of Laughter," *Psychoanalytic Quarterly*, 1950. A psychological explanation of laughter.

Bronson, Bertrand H. Studies in the Comic. Berkeley and Los Angeles: *University of California Press*, 1941. Vol. 8, No. 2 in the University of California Publications in English series, this volume includes Gay's *The Beggar's Opera* among the works of comic literature examined.

Cannon, Gilbert. **Satire**. New York, 1915.

Cook, Albert S. The Dark Voyage and the Golden Mean. Cambridge, Mass., 1949. A standard study of the comic in literature.

Corrigan, Robert W. Comedy: Meaning and Form. San Francisco: Chandler, 1965. A useful anthology which presents theories about the nature of comedy from Aristotle to the present.

Draper, John W. "The Theory of the Comic in Eighteenth-Century England," *Journal of English and German Philology*, XXXVII (1938), pp. 207–223. In reviewing contemporary statements about comedy, Draper concludes that the eighteenth-century theory of comedy followed the tenets of the neo-classical desire to ridicule, but that in practice the tendency was a movement toward sentimentalism.

Eberhart, Richard. "Tragedy as Limitation: Comedy as Control and Resolution," *Tulane Drama Review*, 1962.

Ferenczi, Sandor. *The Psychoanalysis of Wit and the Comical, Further Contributions to Psychoanalysis*, London, 1950.

Freud, Sigmund. "Wit and Its Relation to the Unconscious," trans. A. A. Brill, *Basic Writings of Sigmund Freud*. New York: Modern Library, 1938. Freud really began the investigation of wit and laughter from a psychological point of view.

Frye, Northrop. "The Argument of Comedy," *English Institute Essays*. New York, 1949. An interesting view of comedy in terms of stereotypes or archetypes having an anthropological basis.

Greig, J. Y. *The Psychology of Laughter and Comedy*. London, 1923.

Hazlitt, William. *The English Comic Writers*. New York: E. P. Dutton, 1910. An examination of English comic literature, including *The Beggar's Opera*.

Lauter, Paul, ed. *Theories of Comedy*. New York, 1964. Another anthology of explanations of the comic.

Piddington, Ralph. *The Psychology of Laughter*. London, 1933.

Potts, L. J. *Comedy*. New York, 1963.

Tave, M. Stuart. *The Amiable Humorist*. Chicago, 1960. A study of comic theory and criticism in the eighteenth and nineteenth centuries.

Thorndike, *A. H. English Comedy*. New York, 1929.

Vexler, Julius. "The Essence of Comedy," *Sewanee Review*, 1935.

Wimsatt, W. K., Jr. "The Criticism of Comedy," English Stage Comedy: English Institute Essays, 1954. New York: Columbia University Press, 1955.

Drama

Avery, Emmett L., ed. *The London Stage: A Critical Introduction*. Carbondale: *Southern Illinois University Press*, 1968. Includes essays by E. L. Avery, A. H. Scouten, G. W. Stone, Jr., and C. B. Hogan, all specialists in this field. Especially useful for an understanding of the historical conditions under which eighteenth-century dramas were performed.

Barnet, Sylvan, Morton Berman, and William Burto. *A Dictionary of Literary Terms*. Boston: Little, Brown, 1960. One of several such dictionaries; helpful for the student with a limited technical vocabulary.

Dobree, Bonamy. *Restoration Comedy*. Oxford, 1924. An older study of comedy of the Restoration period which is now under critical attack which is interesting as a background for understanding the dramatic traditions which preceded *The Beggar's Opera*.

Evans, Sir Ifor. *A Short History of English Drama*. Boston: Houghton, Mifflin, 1965 (revised). A quick look at the history of English drama, good for an overall feeling and chronological purposes, but like any volume of this sort, it suffers from generalizing at times.

Ford, Boris. ed. *From Dryden to Johnson. London:* Penguin, 1957. Vol. 4 of the Pelican Guide to English Literature series. Although limited by the amount of territory covered, it is useful for an overall view, and goes into somewhat more detail regarding individual authors than do similar studies.

Fujimura, Thomas H. *The Restoration Comedy of Wit*. Princeton, 1952. An examination that Restoration comedy was used to attack moral issues of the time in a witty rather than sober manner. Again, useful for getting a better perspective on how Gay differed from those who went before him.

Lynch, Kathleen. *The Social Mode of Restoration Comedy*. Ann Arbor, 1926. A study of the influences which helped shape comedy before Gay.

Nicoll, Allardyce. *A History of English Drama, 1660–1900*. Vols. I, II, and III. Cambridge, Mass., 1952–59. A standard literary history, the first three volumes deal with the period from 1660 to 1800. Nicoll comments on individual dramatists, plays, staging, and acting, and includes bibliographies of the dramatists.

____*The Development of the Theatre*. New York: Harcourt, Brace 1958 (revised).

____*The English Theatre. A Short History*. New York, 1936.

Wilson, John Harold. *Preface to Restoration Drama*. Boston, 1965. A very good picture of performance conditions during the reign of Charles II, many of which were still true at Gay's time.

Eighteenth-Century Drama

Bateson, F. W. *English Comic Drama, 1700–1750*. Oxford, 1925. A standard study of British comic drama contemporary with Gay.

Boas, Frederick S. *An Introduction to Eighteenth-Century Drama, 1700–1790*. Oxford University Press: London, 1953. A standard examination of English drama during Gay's time.

Genest, John. *Some Account of the English Stage from the Restoration in 1660 to 1830*. 10 vols. Bath, 1832. Interspersed with critical commentary and limited because it includes only about half of the performances given during this period, Genest's chronological history of stage performances is interesting for the material covered.

Gray, Charles Harold. *Theatrical Criticism in London to 1795*. New York, 1931. A well-documented study of trends in critical taste.

Krutch, Joseph Wood. *Comedy and Conscience after the Restoration*. New York, 1926 (reprinted 1949 and 1967). A standard historical study of the relationship between eighteenth-century comedy and eighteenth-century life, including behavior and conditions in the playhouses.

Loftis, John. *Comedy and Society from Congreve to Fielding*. Stanford University Press: Stanford, 1959. An important examination of the relationship between the presentation of stereotypes and plots and shifts in the English social classifications in the early eighteenth century.

____ *The Politics of Drama in Augustan England.* Oxford, 1963. A study of how English political thought and action were reflected on stage.

Lynch, James L. *Box, Pit, and Gallery: Stage and Society in Johnson's London. University of California Press*: Berkeley and Los Angeles, 1953.

Nettleton, George H. *English Drama of the Restoration and Eighteenth Century.* New York, 1914. A valuable standard examination of the types of plays presented during the eighteenth century, though now somewhat dated.

____, Arthur E. Case, and George Winchester Stone, Jr., eds. *British Dramatists from Dryden to Sheridan.* New York: Houghton Mifflin, 1969. Standard college textbook which examines various types of drama in the eighteenth century and includes representative plays.

Nicoll, Allardyce. *A History of Early Eighteenth-Century Drama, 1700–1750. Cambridge University Press*, 1929. A standard literary history of the period.

Van Lennep, W. B., E. L. Avery, A. H. Scouten, George Winchester Stone, Jr., and C. B. Hogan, eds. *The London Stage, 1660–1800, A Calendar of Plays, Entertainments, and After-pieces, together with Casts, Box-receipts, and Contemporary Comment. II vols.* Carbondale, 1960–1969. An invaluable collection of material for those interested in English stage history.